THE
RISE AND FALL
OF THE SEVERN
BRIDGE RAILWAY
1872–1970

THE
RISE AND FALL
OF THE SEVERN
BRIDGE RAILWAY

An Illustrated History

R.M. Huxley

ALAN SUTTON &
GLOUCESTERSHIRE COUNTY LIBRARY
1984

The County Library Series is published jointly by Alan Sutton
Publishing Limited and Gloucestershire County Library. All correspondence relating to the series should be addressed to:

Alan Sutton Publishing Limited
17a Brunswick Road
Gloucester GL1 1HG

First published 1984

BRITISH LIBRARY CATALOGUING IN PUBLICATION DATA

Huxley, Ron
  The rise and fall of the Severn Railway Bridge 1872–1970.
  1. Severn Bridge (Gloucestershire : Railroad bridge)
  624'.37'09421   TG64.S4

  ISBN 0-86299-120-X

Typesetting and origination by
Alan Sutton Publishing Limited.
Photoset Melior 11/12.
Printed in Great Britain.

Contents

Acknowledgements

The Author is indebted to the following persons for their kind assistance and co-operation during his research into the history of the Severn Bridge Railway.

British Rail, Western Region, for the repoduction of photographs, maps and engineering drawings, etc. Mr. J.E. Tyrer, district civil engineer, Western Region, Gloucester, who kindly allowed access to his files and an office in which to work and to the following personnel of his department, Mr. B. Day, Mr. Vic Harris, Mr. Bloomfield and Mr. Fergus, C. Scoon, the drawing office personnel and the good lady who supplied refreshments.

Mr. F.R.R. Barnwell, chief civil engineer, Western Region, Paddington, for his kind attention to his repeated requests for photographs.

Mr. W.R. Sparrow and the authors of Report E.140 British Transport Commission Research Department, Derby.

Mr. B. Gallagher, Western Region, public relations department.

The Librarian and assistants of the City Library, Gloucester, who kindly allowed the construction photographs to be reproduced.

The Archivist and assistants of the County Records Office, Gloucester.

Mr. F.T.V. Symans, the Guild Hall Custodian, and Mr. P. Preece, the City Swordbearer, who assisted in locating the portrait of W.C. Lucy and allowed its reproduction.

Mr. L.W. Haines, chief engineer, of the Severn River Authority, Malvern, and Mr. Russell Adams, F.R.P.S. for the aerial photographs.

Mr. Dennis Frone, A.R.P.S. for photographic reproduction and Mr. G. Freke for processing.

Messrs. D. Knight, V. Harris, F.C. Scoon, C. Savage, J. Hodges, R. Lane, G. Jones, The Press Association, and J. Ashford for supplying photographs.

Joyce, his wife, who gave up her leisure hours to type the draft of the Manuscript and to Miss Margaret Howe who typed the final copy.

Last, but in no way least, to his good friend Harry Paar, the author of *Severn & Wye Railway* and *The G.W.R in Dean* for his interest, guidance and encouragement, and for kindly providing the introduction to this publication.

Author's Notes

My first journey over the Severn Bridge took place at the tender age of three weeks, when, having been born prematurely while my mother was on holiday at her sister's home at Berkeley, I returned to my parent's home at Blakeney.

Later there came what can be called a twice-yearly pilgrimage to the place of my birth and when in my teens my long school summer holidays were spent at Berkeley. When allowed to ride a cycle I rode down to Sharpness Docks where my uncle, the late Maurice Palmer, worked, and spent endless hours on voyages of discovery around the docks, the lunch time was always spent in the hold of the grain elevator "Leitrim" where there was usually a cask of cider to wash down the sandwiches.

Summer brought scenes of great activity to the banks of the Severn, picnics at Wheel Rock, Purton, beneath the shadows of the bridge; Sunday evening trips to Weston-super-Mare via the bridge, leaving Lydney at 4.00 pm. and arriving back at midnight, all for the princely sum of 1s 3d return.

Thrice yearly P & A Campbells steamers left Sharpness for Ilfracombe calling at Clevedon and Weston, an all round trip of twelve hours. It was on such voyages as this that many of us lads had our first taste of the "demon drink" when we made our way to the bar below and furtively gulped down a half of bitter. the fare was 6/-.

The Severn Bridge was the subject of many local stories some true, like the one concerning Dan Morse an old railway workman who was, on one occasion walking along the track at Severn Bridge Station, an American visitor was waiting for the train to Berkeley and called out to Dan, "Hey sir, this is a fine bridge you have here!" Dan looked up at the platform then back at the bridge and in best Forest dialect replied "Good God! 'im wasn't there yesterday".

Local salmon fisherman Jimmy Legg boasted that he could dive off the highest span fully attired in his salmon fishing gear, lave net over his shoulder and surface with a salmon in the net, – no-one witnessed this event.

The tanker accident turned the clock back eighty years re-opening a great gulf between the east and west banks, but on that night in October

1960 over thirty workmen employed by Fairfields in modifying the bridge owe their lives to the fact that Henry Cooper was fighting the German Karl Muller and by some strange act of fate they opted to take their evening break to coincide with the fight and when the tankers struck they were were safe at Severn Bridge Station listening to the fight being broadcast on the radio, most of the men were working on the two spans that fell prior to the accident.

Many people entertain 'great fears having to cross bridges especially those with no supporting columns below the roadway today they are fearful in crossing the Severn Road Bridge. Keeling's bridge had its problems with cracks in the piers and was both weight and speed restricted but failed from the commercial aspect, it was once referred to as 'white elephant' by a shareholder 101 years ago; do we have another white elephant at Beachley? — only time will answer that question.

R.M. Huxley, A.M.I.E., Eng: Tech: (C.E.I.)

Introduction

As the first bridge across the Severn estuary was being dismantled, the second was being built lower down the river. The new road suspension bridge is not in any sense the victor of a competitive struggle with its old railway counterpart. Railway politics, industrial vicissitudes, and the tunnel lurking below the river bed, had all conspired to reduce its bow-string spans to a low degree of utility, long before. Yet ironically, as the reader will learn, when in 1960 two drifting barges administered the fatal blow, the bridge was in process of being strengthened to take heavier traffic; ironically again, the present road bridge was envisaged half-a-century before the railway bridge was built – in 1825 the *Hereford Journal* noted that 'Telford advised a suspension bridge at Beachley'.

Wise historians regard each work as one in a series of stepping stones to an enlarged knowledge of their subject, rather than the last words on it. To the present writer therefore, who dealt with the Severn railway bridge only as one feature of the Dean Forest railway story, it is a pleasure to introduce this extended account of the 'iron string', as Keeling once referred to his greatest work.[1] The Severn bridge was more than once linked with that of its contempory, the first Tay bridge; but whereas the Tay failed structurally, and quickly, the subject of this book failed commercially, and protractedly. It helped to bankrupt the firm which built it, its owners in fifteen years, and those who tried to demolish it in the end. Yet it did play a useful part in the Severn transport scene, and for eighty years withstood the tide-rip and winds of the great river estuary and the ships which through the years seemed to be attracted magnetically to its piers whenever they got out of control.

Bridges represent one of man's earliest refinements of geography, enabling him to move about more conveniently, and like all his works they deserve a place in the annals of history. The author has given us a detailed account of the erection, use and passing of one of the greatest bridges of its day; drama, courage, patience and frustration will be found in the pages which follow.

Harry Paar
September 1972

CHAPTER ONE

The Schemes that Failed 1810–1872

For more than half-a-century prior to the opening of the Severn Bridge, proposals more or less practicable, were brought before the public for crossing the river either by a bridge or tunnel; and, but for one exception, none of them proceeded further than the stage of incubation. That exception was the scheme for a tunnel under the river near Newnham-on-Severn in 1810.

This scheme met with sufficient support to induce its promoters to form a Company and commence work, but after the excavations had been carried well under the bed of the river, the water broke in, and the men who were working on the project at the time had a narrow escape from drowning; ironically, the date of the flooding was Friday 13 November 1812. Investigations showed the damage to be irreparable and the undertaking was abandoned.

The work on the tunnel commenced on the west bank of the river, in a field midway between Newnham church and Bullo Pill; here a shaft was sunk to the workings, traces of which can still be seen today, and although heavily overgrown and almost filled with debris, the masonry lining is still exposed.

Other schemes for a river crossing were talked of and ended abruptly; but in 1844, the interest of the public was greatly aroused by a proposal made by Isambard Kingdom Brunel when laying out the then projected South Wales Railway.

With the view of making the London and South Wales route as short as possible, Brunel proposed to avoid the detour via Gloucester by crossing the Severn at, or near Awre, carrying the railway in a nearly straight line across the Severn Vale to the Stroud valley where the main line to London was nearly completed.

The notice of application to Parliament in the ensuing session, for a Bill authorising the construction of the South Wales Railway, was published in the *Gloucester Journal* in November 1844. The plans which were published soon afterwards gave another illustration of Brunel's love of the stupendous. A canal was to be cut from the points of the great horseshoe bend of the river at Hock Crib and Framilode Passage, with a capacious lock at each extremity. Over this canal, the railway was to be carried by a swing-bridge, with another swing-bridge

William Charles Lucy – the portrait presented by his friends to the City of Gloucester.
Author's Collection

over the Gloucester and Berkeley Canal, close to its junction with the Stroudwater Canal. At the horseshoe peninsula, (an island that would be formed had the scheme been carried out) a divergence was to take place with one line passing over the river northwards towards Hereford and the main line turning to the south and crossing the river opposite Awre.

These crossings were to made by bridges, one 780 yards and one 800 yards in length. The bridges were to be constructed from timber and the distance between piers fifty-seven feet, with a clear navigation height above high water of twenty-two feet, and forty-two feet at low water.

2

The seal or crest of the Severn Bridge Railway Company, a beautiful copper engraving on a brass mount shows the busy Severn scene.

Author's Collection

The object of the canal with its swing-bridge was to allow river traffic, in those days quite intensive, to proceed up or down the river without hindrance. In the Bill, powers were sought to sell the canal to the Severn Commission, and to enable the Commission to appropriate to the formation and maintenance of the canal, a portion of the tolls recoverable by them under the Severn Commission Act.

If this scheme had been adopted, Gloucester would have been excluded altogether from the main line between London and South Wales, and also with some effect on shipping.

The businessmen of Gloucester were fully alive to this objection to the proposal and did not fail to bring all the influence they could muster to ensure that this railway should be brought into the city. Some months before the scheme had been made public, the surveys made in the district, indicated the intentions of the promoters of the railway, and the Corporation warned the Lords of the Admiralty against the obstruction of the free navigation of the Severn, by the erection of the bridge below Gloucester. As soon as the details of the scheme were known, another memorandum was dispatched to their Lordships, and also to the Board of Trade.

Early in 1845, a public meeting of the citizens of Gloucester was held with resolutions passed to the same effect, and preparations made to oppose the Bill in Parliament. The Board of Trade reported in favour of the scheme and the Lords of the Admiralty, who had jurisdiction over the lower reaches of the river below Gloucester, sent Mr. J.S. Walker, an engineer, to inspect the river at the site of the proposed crossings and to take evidence from local traders as to the effect which the bridges would have on navigation. Walker reported very strongly against the scheme, a line which hardened the hearts of their Lordships. The result was that the House of Commons Committee before whom the Bill came, said that although the preamble of the Bill was proved, the success of the whole scheme entirely depended upon that part of the work to which the Admiralty objected, that they could not consent to proceed with the investigation of a measure which the promoters had not the power of accomplishing, and the Bill was then forgotten.

The main line from London to Gloucester was opened on 12 May 1845, and the advantages of making the South Wales line a continuation of the line to Gloucester, was strongly urged during the proceedings. But with a stubborn obstinacy which seemed inexplicable, the scheme promoted by the South Wales Railway in the following year contained all the objections of the defeated project.

The Company persevered in their scheme for a single bridge,[1] moving the intended site some 200 yards further upstream, and the canal project was omitted. Like the previous scheme, the bridge was to be wooden construction, now fifty-four feet above the high water mark with spans of 100 feet and a total length of 858 yards.

In the meantime the Company had also deposited plans for an alternative line with a tunnel under the river, should permission not be granted for a bridge. The tunnel was to be at Hock Crib and from the commencement in the Parish of Fretherne to its termination in the Parish of Awre, would be one-and-a-half miles long with additional cuttings one mile long. Shortly after the particulars of the scheme was promulgated, Captain Berkeley M.P. wrote to the Lords of the Admiralty on the matter and received a reply assuring him that their Lordships would never sanction a bridge at Hock Crib, or over any other part of the Severn which would be detrimental to the navigation of the river.

The result of this correspondence was that the Company abandoned the proposal for a bridge and persisted in their application for a tunnel. But the House of Commons Committee considered the evidence given before them in favour of the tunnel was insufficient to warrant them in approving it, and the whole part of the Bill referring to crossing the river, was struck out.

A meeting of the Proprietors of the Company was then held and the

Bill was altered to make the South Wales line a continuation of the line then projected into the Forest of Dean. This Bill received Parliamentary sanction, and on 19 September 1851, the South Wales Railway to Chepstow, was opened.

Simultaneously, with the publication of the Parliamentary notice of the second South Wales Railway scheme in the *Gloucester Journal* in November 1845, there appeared a notice of application to Parliament for authority to erect a high level bridge across the Severn at Aust. This bridge was designed by Thomas Fulljames, C.E. of Gloucester and was to have an elevation of approximately 150 feet above high water. A part of the structure was to be built from stone and the two centre spans were to be suspended; the structure was to be of sufficient width to offer a double passage, one for a railway and one for a road. However, the scheme did not proceed past the design stages.

After the passing of the Bill for constructing the South Wales Railway up to the year 1865, several schemes were mooted for the crossing of the river by railway and other purposes between Portskewet and Newnham-on-Severn, all being eventually dropped or failing to achieve Parliamentary sanction.

The year 1865 saw an increase in the mania for constructing new local railways and during the year, no less than four schemes appeared for crossing the river. One was a tunnel to connect the Bristol and South Wales railways below Chepstow, the other was a high level bridge near Chepstow, designed by John Fowler and Hamilton H. Fulton; and the two others were for lines crossing the river by bridges near Newnham-on-Severn, to connect the South Wales Railway with the existing Great Western and Midland line at Stonehouse.

The tunnel project, known as the South Wales Junction scheme[2] was a tunnel four miles long with two air shafts in mid tunnel; the air shafts raised considerable objections and the engineer (Charles Richardson of Bristol) agreed to the re-siting of the shafts, one on each bank of the river.

The high level bridge was part of the proposed South Wales and Great Western Direct Railway[3] running from Chepstow to Wootton Bassett. The river was to be crossed at Oldbury Sand, the bridge being 1,131 yards long, consisting of eighty arches; the main channel was to be crossed by three arches, one 600 feet long and two of 265 feet, the headway being ninety-five feet above high water. Dimensions of the remainder of the arches were to be thirty arches of 150 feet span, fifty feet high; twenty-six of 120 feet span, sixteen feet high; twenty-seven of ninety feet span, fourteen feet high. All in all a massive project.

The Monmouth, Forest of Dean and Standish Junction scheme[4] was

5

practically Brunel's old scheme for crossing the river at Hock Crib, revived, providing a bridge 693 yards long, ten feet above high water, with an opening to allow the passage of vessels. The Severn Junction scheme[5] was for a railway from Stonehouse to Newnham-on-Severn, with a bridge crossing the river just below Newnham. The bridge was to be 2,000 feet long, consisting of eighteen arches, twelve being fifty feet above high water and six being sixty-eight above high water.

The publication of the Parliamentary notices of the schemes in November 1864, was the signal for the start of an organised opposition on the part of local traders. Fowler's high level bridge being regarded with the greatest amount of disfavour because of its impediment to navigation in the lower reaches of the Severn, owing to its insufficient height to allow the larger vessels to proceed upstream, and the large number of piers favouring the accumulation of sand and silting up of the river. The other schemes encountered similar objections, except for the tunnel, which met with the favour of the Bristol merchants; neither was it opposed by Gloucester.

To the other schemes, Gloucester led in opposition. Early in January 1865, Gloucester Chamber of Commerce passed resolutions in opposition to them; and Worcester Chamber of Commerce, after hearing the explanations of Alderman W. Nicks and Philip Cooke, representing Gloucester Corporation and Gloucester Chamber of Commerce respectively, decided to follow their example. The Gloucester Town Council took up the matter heartily and J.P. Heane said it was not a question of the interests but the rights of Gloucester; and parodying the cry adopted during the Reform Bill agitation, he called upon the Council to raise the banner of 'The broad river, the whole broad river and nothing but the broad river'.

A town's meeting was held under the presidency of the Mayor, when it was pointed out in reference to the high level bridge, that for the purpose of shortening the distance between London and South Wales by twenty-one miles, a bridge and a railway would have to be constructed at a cost of more than £2,500,000 and the navigation of the river above Chepstow so seriously impeded, that Gloucester as a port would become nearly extinct. A resolution was passed that the proposed lines for crossing the Severn would be highly prejudicial to the free navigation of the river, which should at all times be scrupulously regarded and had repeatedly been secured by statute, and also injurious to the trade of the port and surrounding districts.

In March, an influential deputation representing public and private traders waited upon the Board of Trade to lay their views to the members of the Board. The deputation was introduced by Sir John

Parkington (later Lord Hampton) and the case of the Corporation, the Gloucester and Berkeley Canal Company, and the Chamber of Commerce was stated by Mr. Powell, who was at the time one of the members for the City. The following extract from the learned member's speech condenses the argument against the schemes.

The Trade of Gloucester amounted to about £3,000,000 per annum and the capital invested at the docks in warehouse, wharves etc., amounted to £1,500,000. Moreover the Gloucester and Berkeley Canal Company had expended £500,000 on the canal. These great interests and the dependent interests of the City itself was seriously imperilled by the new scheme for crossing the river. The first was that called the South Wales and Great Western Direct Railway by which it was intended to cross the river 15 miles below the entrance to the canal at Sharpness Point. At present, this river was the only channel of Gloucester, Worcester and the Midlands Counties to the sea. It was navigable at the point proposed to be crossed, to the extent of 3,963 yards at high water, while even at low water, there were two channels of 30 − 60 fathoms deep. The effect of the proposed scheme, would be to confine the navigable part of the river to one channel and with respect to sea going vessels, to a single arch of 600 feet span. Considering therefore, the tidal influences and currents of the river, it must be obvious that such a bridge would not only be dangerous to all navigation, but would obstruct the larger and more important vessels altogether. The greatest height proposed for the arches was 95 feet and this at certain times of the year, would be reduced from 85 to 82 feet, yet a vessel of over 500 tons, after lowering her main top gallant mast, would still require 100 feet of headway to ensure her passage, so that the proposed amount of headway would be altogether inadequate, especially as the tendence in late years had been in the use of much larger vessels.

Powell proceeded at some length to outline the objections to the schemes, armed with relevent data regarding tonnage of shipping, navigating both the river and the Canal.

The reply given by Milner Gibson of the Board of Trade was that the Board were as much alive as the deputation, to the importance of preserving the navigation of the river and that bearing that object in view, the whole subject should receive their most serious consideration. Subsequently a further memorandum from the Board of Trade was published suggesting alterations, and in consequence amended plans for the high level bridge were submitted. According to the plans originally submitted, the bridge was to have a headway of ninety-five feet above high water at the spring tides; the amended plan provided for a headway of one hundred feet for the three largest arches.

The high level bridge and Severn Junction schemes were referred to referees and the enquiry lasted for more than a month. Early in May, the Monmouth, Forest of Dean and Standish Junction scheme was withdrawn and there was no opposition to the tunnel project. On 17 May, the referees issued their report with reference to the high level bridge and Severn Junction schemes. With reference to the former scheme, the referees reached the following conclusions:–

> As regards the restriction of the waterway, the Referees have not been led to conclude that any material addition to the dangers of the Severn as any inconvenience too great to be reasonably imposed upon those who make use of the navigation would be occasioned by the proposed structure, in case the general interest of the public justify interference. It would add to the risk of the river in times of bad weather and fog and possibly interfere with navigation during the night, a practice which is said to be occasionally resorted to by small vessels. Some inconvenience might also be caused to vessels beating against a headwind and standing out over the sands. The additional dangers which might arise from these causes, do not, however, appear to be serious.
>
> The position of the bridge in a straight reach of some length and in a part of the river where the channel appears from the chart to have remained constant, is favourable for the purpose. The span of the main arch, 600 feet, exceeds that of any bridge in the kingdom and is considerably wider than the actual channel in some other navigable rivers, and, assuming the use of lights and other suitable precautions, the risk of collision with the piers does not appear to justify serious apprehensions. As regards the headway, assuming as it appears fair to do on the balance of evidence, the minimum period of one hour before high water as the time at which vessels going upstream would reach the site of the bridge, the available headway at spring tides would range from 104 feet 3 inches to 100 feet 5 inches, according to the height of the tides. The former figure is calculated from the highest tide ever observed of late years. It is admitted on the part of the promoters that vessels beyond a certain size, which may be taken as 400 tons register, could not pass without lowering their top gallant masts. The evidence is very conflicting as to the existing practice in this respect and also to the

8

degree of inconvenience and delay involved in the operation. Upon the whole, the Referees are led to believe that the masters of the vessels going up to Gloucester seldom lower their masts and they feel considerable repugnance if compelled to do so. Under certain circumstances, with a short crew and under pressure to save a tide, the obligation would probably be inconvenient and it might seriously be so in the case of vessels of large burden when the top of a spring tide might be incurred. On the other hand, it is enforced as a rule in some harbours, and was so, until within a few years at Gloucester. It is necessarily done at the Menai Straits, where the height of the Britannia Bridge is 100 feet above the ordinary spring tides. It was proved to the Referees that this bridge has not prevented the resort to the Port of Caernarvon of vessels of as large a tonnage as those that now go to Gloucester. Though the practice may involve some trouble and occasionally delay, it cannot be regarded as a serious impediment to navigation.

The Referees were of the opinion, that if this proposed new communication should be considered to afford important advantages to the public, the objections which had been raised upon engineering grounds, were not such as to justify the rejection of the scheme. In regard to the Severn Junction scheme, the Referees were of the opinion that should the Committee allow it to proceed, the promoters should be legally bound to construct the second arch of the bridge from the western shore, of a span of 300 feet and the third arch of a span of 180 feet, and that should this requirement be carried out, there would be no engineering objections to the construction of the proposed bridge.

The two Bills came before the House of Commons Committee on 18 May and although they were strenuously opposed, they were passed on 26 May. On 30 June, the Bills passed the Committee of the House of Lords and received Royal Assent on 5 July.

Four months after the schemes received Royal Assent, in November 1865, Parliamentary notice was given of two other schemes for crossing the river at Gatcombe, the adoption of either, of which, it was urged, would give advantages over Fowler's scheme at Chepstow, causing no interference with the navigation of the river to the entrance of the Gloucester and Berkeley Canal. Both schemes proposed to connect the South Wales line at Lydney with the Great Western line at Stonehouse and the Midland line at Frocester.

The Midland and South Wales Junction Railway[6] proposed to cross the river at Tites Point to near Gatcombe and the Midland and Great

Western Juction Railway[7] proposed to cross at more or less the same point. In January 1866, the two schemes were referred to the engineers of the Midland, Great Western and South Wales Railway Companies and the result was that ultimately both were abandoned. In November of the same year, notice was given of the intention of the promoters of Fowler's high level bridge, to apply for an extension of time for the purchase of land and the completion of works, but it need hardly be said that Fowler's high level scheme, the Severn Junction and the tunnel schemes, after being before the public for some considerable time, were finally abandoned.

The question of bridging the Severn, remained in abeyance until 1870, when two more projects appeared on the horizon, one being a tunnel beneath the river at Portskewett, the object of which was to connect the railways running through the Welsh coalfields with the existing railway in the Bristol area, viz., the Bristol and South Wales Union Railway, then serving the New Passage Ferry, the other for a bridge (for road as well as railway traffic) at Purton. with a broad and narrow gauge railway system connecting the Severn & Wye and South Wales railways with the Midland and Great Western, with a short line or branch to the then proposed new docks at Sharpness, the latter being known as the Severn Junction scheme[8], engineered by G.W. Keeling and G. Wells Owen. Unlike its predecessors, the scheme was supported by the commercial interests of Gloucester, because of the impetus it would give to trade. The House of Commons Committee were also highly favourable to it, but the scheme finally collapsed in consequence of no satisfactory financial evidence being forthcoming.

The collapse of the scheme from such a cause, was the source of extreme regret and it was suggested the necessary money might be obtained by a guarantee fund formed by a tonnage rate on the mineral properties of the Forest, certain advantages as to traffic being given in return. But the suggestion was not carried out; the Severn tunnel scheme was abandoned and another year passed without any success-ful attempt to bridge the river.

Near the end of 1871, no less than six schemes, all of which included a passage over the river, came before the public. The *Gloucester Journal* of 2 December 1871 published the following details of the schemes:—

The South Midland Railway[9]:

This line is proposed to run from Lydney, crossing the Severn and via Berkeley Road, Wotton-under-Edge and Oldbury on the Hill to Malmesbury. Here it receives a proposed line from Nailsworth in continuation of the Stonehouse and Nailsworth Railway. From Malmesbury it passes via Wootton Bassett, where it has a junction with the Great Western Railway to Hungerford. Here the line divides, one branch passing to Andover and there join the London and South Western Railway, and the other to the same company's line at Basingstoke. The total length of the through line from Lydney to Andover is 73 miles and five furlongs. The branch lines make up a further mileage of 39 miles and 4 furlongs – a total of 113 miles and 1 furlong. There are eighteen tunnels contemplated, fourteen of which are on the through line; these make an aggregate length of 8 miles and 985 yards. The tunnels vary from 3,000 yards and 2,953 yards to 231 yards and 180 yards in length. The gradient from Lydney to the river crossing is 1 in 180, with a tunnel 954 yards long. The bridge is to be 1,351 yards long with 33 spans, two being 300 feet long, 70 feet high, 29 of 100 feet and two of 65 feet, all constructed on a level plane. Gloucester interests, so far as they are concerned in this crossing of the river, are apparently not considered, inasmuch as no communication is proposed to Holly Hazle Docks. (Sharpness.)

The Western Junction Railway[10]

This scheme consists of a bridge over the Severn above Sharpness with two lines running from the Western end of the bridge, one to Lydney and the other linking with the Forest of Dean Central Railway. At the eastern end of the bridge, the line unites itself with the proposed Midland branch to Holly Hazle Docks. In conjunction with the scheme is a road bridge connecting with the turnpike roads on both sides of the river. The line from Lydney, rises by a gradient of 1 in 100, thus dispensing with any tunnel before reaching the river bank, but at the cost of passing over a summit 33 feet higher than the South Midland. The line is to be carried over the Severn, partly on an open viaduct 880 yards long and partly on an embankment, 286 yards long. There are two spans of 300 feet each with 70 feet to 58 feet, with a descending gradient to the Docks of 1 in 100. The total length of the line and branches is $6\frac{1}{2}$ miles. The roadway is proposed to be placed above the railway track on the bridge.

The Severn Bridge Railway No. 2 (Sharpness)[11]

This scheme is identical as to route, with the South Midland and with so much of the Western Junction scheme as passes in the

11

direction of Lydney. The gradient from Lydney to the summit level is 1 in 133 with a tunnel 400 yards in length. The river is crossed by a bridge 1,404 yards long, consisting of two spans 300 feet each and 69 feet high, and 26 spans of 100 feet each with an average headway of 57 feet. A roadway is also proposed as in the previously mentioned scheme. From the summit level at the tunnel the line descends to the Docks by a gradient of 1 in 137. A branch line is proposed to Holly Hazle Docks; by which respect the scheme differs from its competitors. The branch leaves the main line shortly after crossing the river and crosses the inland entrance to the New Docks and thence along the rear of the dock property on the north western side, where sidings and conveniences will be provided to carry on a large export trade. An additional advantage is claimed for this scheme by reason of a power which has been sought for the county to contribute to the maintenance of the carriage road. In former years, proposals for roads have been abandoned for the reason that although a great public boon, they would give no return for the necessary outlay. This scheme avoids that objection by enabling the county rate to aid in supporting the road, which, in the case of other important bridges in the country, is a liability sustained entirely by the county rate.

The total length of the line and its branches is 5½ miles.

The Severn Bridge Railway No. 1 (Beachley)[12]:

This line commences by a junction with the South Wales Railway at a point one chain east of Chepstow bridge and thence to Beachley Point, crossing the river by a viaduct 1,780 yards long, carried on 27 spans of the following dimensions:— two of 800 feet each with a headway of 95 feet, one of 250 feet, 6 of 160 feet each and 18 of 150 feet each; the headway in the lesser spans varying between 95 feet and 75 feet. The viaduct joins the Gloucestershire shore at Aust Cliff, where the line enters in a cutting of 23 feet, a gradient of 1 in 100 followed by two miles of level track, bringing the line to its termination, by a junction with the Bristol and South Wales Union Railway, about three quarters of a mile east of Pilning station. The worst gradient on the line against a load from South Wales is 1 in 150. At Aust Cliff a branch is proposed to the Midland Railway at Thornbury; There are two other branches to junctions with the South Wales line and the authorised Wye Valley Railway.

The Severn Tunnel Railway[13]

This proposed line commences by a junction with the Bristol and South Wales Union Railway, about six furlongs east of Pilning station and then descends by a gradient of 1 in 100 for approximately three miles until beneath the area of the river known as 'The Shoots'. Here two shafts about 500 yards apart are proposed to be placed in the waterway for the purpose of ventilation, the tunnel at this point being 53 feet below the river bed. It then ascends to the Monmouthshire side by a gradient of 1 in 100, the total length of the tunnel being 7,040 yards long of which 3,000 yards are under land, the remainder being beneath the river. The line terminates by a junction with the South Wales Railway, about three miles below Portskewett station and is 7 miles 7 furlongs in length.

The Severn Bridge Railway (Portskewett)[14]:

This scheme commences with a junction with the South Wales Railway at a point about a mile west of Portskewett station. Ascending by a gradient of 1 in 88, it reaches the river in about one mile, the gradient continues until the summit is reached at a point over 'The Shoots'; here the line is carried by a span of 700 feet across the navigation channel and with a headway of 100 feet above high water at spring tides. The line then descends by a gradient of 1 in 100, until the Gloucestershire shore is reached and thence to its junction with the Bristol and South Wales Union Railway, approximately one mile from New Passage station. The viaduct over the river is 3,920 yards in length, its spans being one of 700 feet, two of 350 feet each, 42 of 150 feet each and 26 of 100 feet each, a total of 71 spans. The length of the railway is 4 miles and 3 furlongs.

The South Midland Railway scheme received a great deal of local support, but the Canal Company, the Gloucester Chamber of Commerce and most of the private traders, were strongly in favour of the Sharpness bridge scheme. The engineers for this scheme were George William Keeling and G. Wells Owen; both were members of the Institute of Civil Engineers. Keeling and Owen, who had been engaged in making a survey of the river in 1859, had carefully studied the question and had arrived at the conclusion that the best and most economical site for a bridge was near Purton Passage, where, owing to the configuration of the river, the channel never varied and good

13

foundations could be obtained at a reasonable depth. Moreover, the site was above the entrance to the Gloucester and Berkeley Canal and would therefore, only affect the navigation of smaller craft proceeding to Bullo Pill Docks.

The South Midland Railway scheme was abandoned in January 1872, sufficient support had not been forthcoming to warrant the promoters in further proceeding with the scheme at the present time.

Early in February, the Severn Bridge Railway Bill (Sharpness) passed the Standing Orders Committee and in the beginning of the following month, the Board of Trade presented their report to the House of Commons upon the four Bills which had been introduced for crossing the Severn, namely, The Severn Bridge Railway No. 1 (Beachley), the Severn Bridge Railway No. 2 (Sharpness), The Severn Tunnel Railway and the Western Junction.

A strong opinion was expressed against the Beachley scheme and on 6 March, the Severn Tunnel Bill received its second reading in the House of Commons. On 22 March the Beachley scheme was withdrawn, and a similar fate terminated the Western Junction Scheme.

References to Chapter One

Gloucester Records Office Plans and books of reference deposited with the Clerk of the Peace.

1.   South Wales Railway   Q Rum 184.
2.   South Wales Junction Railway   Q Rum 332.
3.   South Wales and Great Western Direct Railway   Q Rum 337.
4.   Monmouth Forest of Dean and Standish Junction   Q Rum 328 & 346.
5.   Severn Junction Railway   Q Rum 331.
6.   Midland and South Wales Junction Railway   Q Rum 345.
7.   Midland and Great Western Junction Railway   Q Rum 344.
8.   Severn Junction Railway   Q Rum 368.
9.   South Midland Railway   Q Rum 382.
10. Western Junction Railway   Q Rum 389.
11. Severn Bridge Railway No. 2 (Sharpness)   Q Rum 385.
12. Severn Bridge Railway No. 1 (Beachley)   Q Rum 388.
13. Severn Tunnel Railway   Q Rum 367.
14. Severn Bridge Railway (Portskewett)   Q Rum 384.

This Chapter is based on *The History of previous bridge schemes, Gloucester Journal* 18 October 1879.

CHAPTER TWO

The Objectors

The Passage of the Severn Bridge Railway Bill
(No.2) through Parliament.[1]

The original design of the bridge provided for twenty-eight spans, and as a result of this the project met with some objections from the Severn Commissioners, who were apprehensive that silting up of the navigation channel might occur. After numerous consultations with the designers and the proprietors of the proposed company, the original design was amended to provide larger openings, and it was finally determined that twenty-one spans would be sufficient to overcome these objections.

The Severn Bridge Railway Bill No. 2 came before the Examiners on 7 February 1872. It was opposed by the promoters of the Western Junction Bill, and after a long list of allegations had been discussed, the Examiners decided to report that the standing orders had been duly complied with.

In the case of the Severn Bridge No. 1 Bill, a report of noncompliance was set up and allegations of a serious nature were to be inquired into, when once again the question of interference with the navigation of the river reared its ugly head.

THURSDAY 11 APRIL, FIRST DAY

The Presiding Officer of the Select Committee was Sir Hadworth Williamson, and the other members were Mr. Eaton, Mr. Eykyn and Mr. Somerset Beaumont. Mr. Granville Somerset Q.C., and Mr. Pember appeared on behalf of the promoters. Mr. Pope Q.C., and Mr. Philbrick appeared in opposition on behalf of Lord Fitzhardinge. The following petitioners were also represented: the Severn & Wye Railway and Canal Company by Mr. Cripps Q.C., owners of vessels navigating the Severn by Mr. Thesiger, the Gloucester Commissioner of Sewers and the Great Western and Midland Railway Companies.

The first witnesses appeared on behalf of the promoters; the Hon. J.K. Howard, Commissioner of H.M. Woods and Forests spoke of the advantages of the bridge to both the Forest and the Crown. W.B. Clegram, Engineer to the Gloucester and Berkeley Canal Company gave considerable details of the tonnages of vessels leaving Gloucester and Sharpness empty, stressing the need for more exports. He said he had been connected with docks for forty-four years and was familiar with all the aspects of the river. In his opinion, he did no think the navigation of the river would be seriously affected by the erection of the bridge, and the new docks at Sharpness would be incomplete without it.

The latter witness was severely cross-examined by Philbrick and Thesiger.

W.P. Price, M.P. the chairman of the Midland Railway, S.S. Marling, M.P., and William Charles Lucy, chairman of the proposed Severn Bridge Railway Company, endorsed Clegram's evidence. Lucy stated a resolution in favour of the bridge had been passed by Gloucester Chamber of Commerce, who had also petitioned Parliament in its favour, and Gloucester Corporation was wholly in favour of the scheme. He proceeded to give details of trade up and down the river, and finally, he was cross-examined by Thesiger, his replies completely answering the case thought to be made out by the opposition.

E.L. Kendall, Ship Owner of Gloucester and W. Nicks, Timber Merchant, gave considerable details of imports, and the lack of exports, stressing the need for more exports, as many vessels were leaving Gloucester and Sharpness in ballast.

During the first day's hearing the Great Western Railway did not appear in opposition in the hope of obtaining terms which would, in effect, exclude the Midland Railway Company from the Forest and also keep out the Severn & Wye Railway and Canal Company, but the firm and independent attitude taken up by the directors of the Severn Bridge Railway Company, and the tact shown by the Severn & Wye Railway and Canal Company and their Solicitors defeated the plans of the Great Western Railway.

FRIDAY 12 APRIL, SECOND DAY

When the Committee assembled for the second day, W.P. Price was recalled, and the chairman, querying the failure of the previous scheme in 1870, asked if he, Price, could guarantee that sufficient capital could be raised to meet the outlay of the bridge. Price replied he could not give a simple answer of 'yes' or 'no', but with the consent of the Committee, he would make a statement which would involve the only reply he could give. He gave considerable details which showed that the Midland Railway, and Great Western Railway could not subscribe to the undertaking without each other's consent, and referred to the

Great Western Railway's objections to the scheme, which had appeared only at the last moment; he thought the whole matter should be referred to arbitration, to which the Midland Railway would be perfectly prepared to do.

The chairman raised the question of the directors named in the Bill. He enquired if they were gentlemen, who having put their names to the scheme, would see the project carried out. Price said he was sure this was so, the promoters had made their own deposit amounting to £25,000 and had not put themselves in the hands of bankers to do this. Granville Somerset asked if the £14,000 deposit required under standing orders, was found by the gentlemen named in the Bill. Price replied that they had contributed every shilling of it and made their own contract. Granville Somerset spoke of the 'Bogus' Bill of 1870, which failed because of the lack of responsible persons to back it and asked if this was a bona fide Bill, to which Price replied 'Yes'.

Round then took up the cross-examination of Price and this continued for most of the hearing, with most of Round's questions confined to the financial backing of the Bill. Finally, the chairman remarked that he was fully satisfied with the replies given and the other members of the committee were also satisfied.

J.A. Grahame Clarke and G.B. Keeling of the Severn & Wye Railway and Canal Company gave evidence concerning new extensions to their railway, viz., extensions at Lydbrook to join the Ross – Monmouth Railway and the accommodation at Lydney. Keeling was cross-examined for some time, mostly on the question of railway management. Thomas Sully of the Parkend Coal Company told the Committee that his company shipped 95,000 tons of coal per annum from Lydney Harbour, and he gave facts and figures on the cost of shipping coal to the west of England.

H.R. Luckes of Newnham-on-Severn, said that as a former banker of the Forest of Dean and Director of the Ross & Monmouth Railway, he had given much consideration to the railway accommodation of the Forest of Dean. As a colliery and iron ore owner, he had done all within his power to bring about better railway facilities to the area. He thought the bridge would open up better routes for both passengers and the mineral wealth of the Forest. The witness was cross-examined by Pope, Round and Granville Somerset regarding the Bristol and Radstock coalfields.

At the conclusion of the evidence, the Chairman said that he thought it clear that the Forest trade would benefit by the bridge, and the Committee did not want any further evidence regarding the shipments at Lydney.

Thomas Forster Brown informed the Committee he had been a Deputy Gaveller of the Forest of Dean since 1864. The iron ore field of the Forest was 24,000 acres and the coalfield 15,000 acres; he considered there were 300,000,000 tons of unworked coal in the area, but could only guess at the quantity of iron. Since 1864, the output of coal had increased to more than 100,000 tons per year and he thought the bridge was in the best interests of the Crown and Forest. Brown was cross-examined on the technical tenure of the Forest and finally in reply to a question by the committee, said that he did not care so long as all the railways had running powers over the bridge, but he thought it important that the bridge did not get into the hands of the Great Western Railway.

James Allport, general manager of the Midland Railway, informed the committee his company had always looked with favour on any scheme to cross the river and he was cross-examined mainly on arrangements between the different railway companies. In reply to a question from the chairman, he said he had no doubt the railway would be speedily constructed and financed, if the Act was obtained. W. Purcell, a Severn pilot of thirty years experience, very much amused the court by the quaint and clever way in which he gave his evidence, the free use of nautical terms and some smart passages of repartee between himself and the examining counsel, often at their expense, being the main point of the evidence, which proved the bridge would not be an impediment to the navigation of the river. This evidence was also confirmed by William Long and William Clements, two other pilots. G.W. Keeling and G. Wells Owen presented their evidence, dealing mostly with the technical aspects of the scheme and the Committee adjourned for the week-end.

MONDAY 15 APRIL, THIRD DAY

The committee re-assembled and G.W. Keeling was recalled for cross-examination. He said he was the engineer to the Severn & Wye Railway and Canal Company but had received no instructions from the Company with regard to laying out the proposed line. He informed the committee that he acted independently on behalf of the promoters. The proposed railway was for a single track and the bridge would be also for single track, but if traffic would be of an extensive nature, there would be no difficulty in doubling the whole railway, including the bridge.

Pope, cross-examining, referred to Lord Fitzhardinge's petition in that on the previous Friday, Keeling had said that one of the main objects in laying out the bridge was to prevent damage to his Lordship's property. Keeling agreed and Pope asked what damage was envisaged in laying out the bridge. Keeling replied he was anxious to cut as little as possible into his Lordship's property by reason of the deflecting of the tide upon his land. Pope asked what was the effect of the Wheel Rock upon the tide and whether it affected the tide from the opposite shore. Keeling thought it might give some effect on the ebb tide but not on the flood ti le which ran at a velocity of about eight miles per hour. Wheel Rock had no effect in altering the channel and neither would the piers of the proposed bridge. There would be twenty-one piers to the bridge, three of them twenty feet wide and the remainder ten feet wide. There would be a projecting flange of six inches at the low tide level of each pier and although the current would be slower within the cage of each pier, he did not think there would be any silting. During his experience extending over twelve years there had been no variation of the channel at the spot where the bridge would cross. Indeed an Admiralty chart, dated 1814, showed that there had been no alteration since that year. Keeling added that whenever they had made efforts to improve the communications with the Forest of Dean, they had always met with strongest opposition on the part of the Great Western Railway.

George Wells Owen, in reply to Pember, said that he was a civil engineer and in conjuction with Thomas Elliott Harrison and G.W. Keeling, had laid out the bridge. He had known the South Wales district, the Forest of Dean and the Severn, for many years; the width of the river at that particular point was 3,617 feet and the total width of all the bridge piers was 140 feet; that was near as possible four per cent and in his opinion, there would be no silting of the channel and no better spot for erecting a bridge could possibly be selected.

In reply to a question by Round, Wells Owen said that regarding the swing-bridge, it would only be necessary to open it two or three times per day, because the smaller vessels could pass, owing to their shorter masts. The pier on Wheel Rock could be used as a buoy or beacon to show the position of the rock. Thomas Elliott Harrison consulting engineer to the Gloucester and Berkeley Canal Company and acting engineer of the New Docks, gave evidence as to the practicability of the scheme and the sufficiency of the estimate of £275,000. He had constructed the two largest swing-bridges in England, over the Ouse near Goole and York, and his opinion was that no inconvenience or danger would arise from the proposed swing-bridge over the canal and he could not imagine how the remainder of the bridge would affect Lord Fitzhardinge's property. This closed the case for the promoters.

It was then announced that Thesiger, as representative of the owners of vessels who petitioned against the Bill and Pope, the counsel for

Lord Fitzhardinge, had resolved to amalgamate their respective cases, which were in the main, identical.

Mr. Watson, civil engineer of Stoke Court, Berkeley was then called by Thesiger and said that the proposed scheme would cause considerable injury to Lord Fitzhardinge's property.

TUESDAY 16 APRIL, FOURTH DAY

The next witness, Captain Culver stated that there was a similar bridge to the proposed bridge over the Severn, over the River Ouse which had caused great obstruction to the navigation of that river. He was of the opinion that the proposed bridge would practically destroy the navigation between the site and Gloucester.

On being cross-examined by Granville Somerset, Captain Culver said he objected to any bridge being built across the Severn, however, if one was to be constructed, he was of the opinion that the best site would be at Chepstow. He did not think vessels of sixty tons could be taken through the proposed bridge safely, although the span opening was three hundred feet and spoke on this subject as a sailor.

Joseph Warren of Framilode and for twenty years a registered master trading between Bullo Pill and Bridgwater, William Prout, a pilot and ex master of a vessel trading the same route as Warren for the previous thirty-five years, George Williams, and William Matthews, registered and licenced pilots, endorsed the evidence of Captain Culver. John Gower, master mariner and ship owner was called and examined by Philbrick. He said he resided at Framilode and had been master of a vessel navigating up and down the Severn for twenty-three years. He had traded for the past fifteen years from Bullo Pill to a small place in Somerset near Burnham. Near the proposed bridge, namely the Waveridge Sands, there was a very heavy ground swell which welled up without warning and he had known a vessel sink almost immediately in consequence of this and vessels subjected to its influence were rendered perfectly unmanageable. He was of the opinion, that the bridge would add additional hazards to the river, especially when twenty to thirty vessels were proceeding down river on one tide.

Lord Fitzhardinge, the next witness, was questioned by Philbrick. He said he was the owner for life of a considerable estate at Berkeley Castle, which extended down to the river above and below the site of the proposed bridge. He had some 200–300 acres of land situated on the bank of the river, which was some feet below the water level at high tide. This land was protected by embankments and breakwaters which had been kept in a proper state of repair from time immemorial by the owners of the estate. He was under the necessity of employing trust-worthy servants to look after the embankments and on the first indication of a breach being discovered, this had to be repaired immediately, all of which cost considerable amounts of money. He deemed it a matter of the greatest importance to prevent the strong wash of the water against his embankments. Near the Royal Drough Drain the land was ten feet below the level of the regular spring tides, an embankment was constructed at this point with a protecting breakwater. If any obstruction was placed on Wheel Rock, the rock would act as a breakwater and deflect the tide across the river near the Royal Drough Drain with increased velocity which would have an injurious effect on his property.

Lord Fitzhardinge then proceeded to tell the committee of the effects of the bridge on his fishery. He stated he was the owner of a salmon fishery near the site for the proposed bridge, it was called Wheel Rock Fishery, which was let on a long lease to Thomas Pearce for £40 per year. He thought if the bridge was constructed the result would be that all the fish would be driven away from that particular part of the river and therefore completely destroy the value of the fishery. In his opinion, there was no public necessity for the bridge.

On being cross-examined by Granville Somerset, Lord Fitzhardinge said he did not entertain the smallest objection to a bridge being thrown across the river, but he did object to the present Bill because if it succeeded in passing Parliament, the result would be a vast sacrifice of life and property.

G.W. Keeling was recalled and stated that he had looked over the whole of Lord Fitzhardinge's estate and found that reclaimed land in the vicinity of the Royal Drough Drain was nearly on a level with an ordinary spring tide, the level of the high spring tide was three to four feet above the surrounding land.

WEDNESDAY 17 APRIL, FIFTH DAY

On re-assembling, evidence on behalf of Lord Fitzhardinge was given by James Herbert Cooke, principal steward to the Berkeley Castle Estate and Octavious Long. Handel Cosham was questioned by Thesiger regarding the branch line, before Parliament, from Berkeley Road to the New Docks. Cosham stated that the branch, when it was constructed, would afford ample facilities for bringing coal to Sharpness. There would, therefore, be no public necessity for the proposed railway.

Henry Hetheridge, F.R.S. attached to the Royal School of Mines told the committee there were large quantities of coal in the neighbourhood of Bristol and the quality was as good as that in the Forest of Dean. On being cross-examined by Granville Somerset, he remarked that he had no doubt that there was 300,000,000 tones of unmined coal in the Forest and that 24,000 acres of iron ore existed there, but he firmly believed that the Bristol coal would be cheaper in the long run.

James Abernethy, civil engineer, in answer to Pope said he had inspected the site and assuming that a bridge was necessary, was satisfied that a worse site could not have been selected in any part of the river.

Mr. Grierson, general manager of the Great Western Railway, was called and examined by Round. He said there was no necessity for the proposed scheme. In the course of a few months, when the narrow gauge system was completed, the Great Western Railway would be able to convey the mineral produce of the Forest from Lydney to any part of the country on their own system.

The proceedings were terminated after Round had addressed the committee on behalf of the Great Western Railway.

THURSDAY 18 APRIL, SIXTH DAY

Granville Somerset summed up the evidence on behalf of the promoters, who, he remarked, were men of great weight and influence in the locality. Among them were S.S. Marling, M.P. for the Western Division of Gloucester. W.P. Price, M.P. for Gloucester, a warm supporter of the measure, both in his individual capacity and as chairman of the Midland Railway. Many other gentlemen of high position were promoters of the scheme and had enabled the committee to pronounce on the question of finance and shown that the present Bill was not a 'bogus' Bill like the Bill of 1870. He thought that the opposition by the Great Western Railway was merely because it could not obtain exclusive possession of the line, yet even the Great Western Railway could not deny that there was a great necessity for some connection between the Forest and Sharpness.

Lord Fitzhardinge had come forward for the protection of his territory, but many gentlemen who owned land, which would be as much affected as his Lordship's property, offered no opposition to the scheme.

He said the principal object of the Bill was to connect the western and eastern banks of the River Severn for the purpose of supplying the acknowledged deficiency of exports at the docks and to afford an opportunity for the house and steam coal of the Forest to be transported throughout England upon the narrow gauge system.

Sir Hadworth Williamson, interposing, remarked that the contention of the opponents of the Bill was that the export trade could be fed from the Bristol coalfield.

Granville Somerset said that the answer to that was, that although for upwards of forty years, there had been no railway communication with that coalfield, it had not been to any extent proved, besides, the coal was vastly inferior to that of the Forest. If however, Parliament gave the promoters the power of bringing minerals from the Forest of Dean and South Wales to the New Docks, an enormous traffic would be developed. The chairman said if the necessities of the Forest were not sufficient to authorise the scheme, the learned counsel could not make out his case by dwelling on the wants of South Wales.

Granville Somerset remarked that he had put his case both as a local and as a thorough one. He contended that the local necessities were of themselves sufficiently great to warrant the construction of the new line.

The learned counsel then commented at considerable length on the evidence adduced on behalf of the petitioners and terminated his address with an earnest appeal to the committee to declare that the preamble of the Bill had been proved.

Sir Hadworth said the committee would report that the preamble was proved. They were of the opinion, however, that clauses should be inserted giving compensation to Lord Fitzhardinge for any injury which might be sustained to his property by the construction of the bridge. A clause should also be inserted compensating his Lordship for the loss of his salmon fishery.

On Friday, the committee considered the clauses which had been prepared by Granville Somerset and the preamble was found proved.

The Bill found little opposition in the House of Lords and it received Royal Assent[2] on 18 July 1872.

References to Chapter Two

1.   *Gloucester Journal* Saturday 13 April 1872, Saturday 20 April 1872; The Gloucester Collection, City Library
2.   Severn Bridge Railway (No. 2) Act 35 and 36 Vic. C 109

CHAPTER THREE

The Bridge is born 1872–1879

The first meeting of the Severn Bridge Railway Company

On 31 August 1872 the first meeting of the Severn Bridge Railway Company was held at the Canal Office, Gloucester, attended by the directors, Messrs. W.C. Lucy, chairman; W.B. Clegram, vice chairman; S.S. Marling, M.P., E. Crawshay, T.N. Foster, R.W. Freeman, H.M. James, H.R. Luckes and C. Walker, all of which were named in the Severn Bridge Railway Act.

Lucy, in addressing the shareholders said the railway was promoted by gentlemen who were desirous of utilising the existing railway system and not to the opposition of any one existing company.

In endeavouring to accomplish this, they had tried to make amicable arrangements with the two companies affected, the Midland Railway and the Great Western Railway, but he was sorry to say the latter had replied that they could not render any support. However, the Midland Railway were anxious to support the scheme and he felt the Great Western Railway would be equally so on the completion of the bridge.

The Severn Bridge Railway was now about to issue its prospectus for the purpose of taking up the necessary shares to carry out the work, and he would like that the Company would prefer that the shareholders should be personally residing in the locality of the bridge or in Gloucester, rather than persons living at a distance, whose only concern was to receive a good dividend.

The Severn Bridge Railway Company Prospectus

The line of Railway commenced by junctions with the Severn & Wye and Great Western Railways at Lydney, where it crossed the Severn by a bridge and joined the Midland Railway at Sharpness New Docks, thus bringing the Midland Railway into communication with the Severn and Wye Railway, and so to nearly every colliery and iron works in the Forest of Dean, affording the Great Western Railway by means of their existing running powers, a shorter through route from South Wales to London by fourteen miles. The line was also designed to supply the pressing necessities of the trade of the district and afford an improved communication for the large and increasing traffic of the Forest of Dean with the south and south west of England. The railway was approximately five miles long and crossed the river via twenty-one arches at the most favourable point in the river. In the first instance, it was proposed to construct it as a single line, the directors being advised that there would be no difficulty in doubling the line when the traffic required it. Its estimated cost was £277,973. Power was taken to raise £300,000 – £225,000 in shares and £75,000 by loans and to charge three additional miles for the bridge, which was 1,404 yards in length. There would also be a footway over the bridge as a communication of that kind would be much needed by the population on both sides of the river. At Sharpness, there had existed for many years in the past, a considerable trade in coal and timber imported through the Gloucester and Berkeley Canal to the city of Gloucester, where it was despatched by water or rail into the interior. The following statement shows the increase in trade of the port of Gloucester in the previous five years.

	IMPORTS: TONS	EXPORTS: TONS
Five years ending 25 September 1866	1,160,008	253,838
Five years ending 25 September 1871	1,474,294	315,365

The Prospects

From the prospectus, it appeared that taking the previous five years, imports exceeded the exports by an annual average of upwards of 231,000 tons which in the latter year reached 250,000 tons. This excess had risen from the want of a suitable communication between the shipping and the mineral industries of South Wales and the Forest of Dean, the practice being for vessels, when discharged at Sharpness or Gloucester, to take in ballast and proceed to a South Wales or Forest of Dean port for an export cargo, usually of coal or iron.

With all these drawbacks, however, there was an increasing trade at Sharpness and although the directors could only point out an existing annual demand for 250,000 tons of cargo, they confidently anticipated that when the inconveniences were overcome by the opening of the new docks and the construction of the bridge, with the branch of the Midland Railway as well as the connections which would be formed with the Great Western system, a very large accession of trade would speedily follow.

To the Forest of Dean, the railway was admitted to be of first importance, affording access to sea-going shipping at Sharpness and in conjunction with other existing lines, would offer cheaper through routes, avoiding long detours then necessary by the normal routes. Of six schemes proposed, only the Severn Bridge Railway and Severn Tunnel had received Royal Assent. The tunnel project cost was estimated at £750,000 and power had been taken to subscribe £1,000,000 and to charge twelve additional miles for the tunnel.

The distance from South Wales to London via the bridge was practically the same as via the tunnel and a comparison of the gradients favoured the bridge. Should both crossings be completed, the directors of the Severn Bridge Railway were of the opinion that the important mineral traffic to London could be carried via the Severn Bridge, at as low or even lower tolls and with great regularity and despatch as by the Severn Tunnel and that it would consequently command a good portion of through traffic.

They relied, however, on the traffic of the immediate district as the undoubted justification for the line and believed that it alone would be quite adequate to provide a remunerative dividend on the cost of the undertaking; but at the same time, they could not ignore the prospects of the exceptional returns which they believed would result from the accommodation of through traffic.

Parliamentary running powers were sought by and given to the Midland Railway and Great Western Railway which they could exercise on their respectively subscribing a minimum sum of £25,000 each and the shareholders of the Severn & Wye Railway and Canal Company, Gloucester & Berkeley Canal Company, and the Midland Railway Company, in special meetings assembled had given their unanimous approval to the scheme.

Owing to the unsatisfactory condition of the labour market and the high cost of materials, it was decided to defer operations for a time. Considerable further delays arose in consequence of the difficulties arising from conflicting interests. Differences of opinion arose between the Midland Railway and Great Western Railways Companies as to the power of the Midland Railway to contribute towards the undertaking by subscribing £50,000. The matter was referred to arbitration and lingered on for several months but in February 1874, it was announced that the arbitrators had decided in favour of the Midland Railway, and that the Company had determined to subscribe the full amount they were allowed to subscribe under the Act, viz., £50,000. The Gloucester and Berkeley Canal Company had held a special meeting the previous November and a similar sum had been authorised, and shortly afterwards, the Severn and Wye Railway and Canal Company decided to subscribe £25,000 and the great question remained, would the Great Western Railway Company avail themselves of their powers to subscribe a similar sum to that subscribed by the Midland Railway Company?

The Great Western Railway had, in the meantime, decided to proceed with the tunnel project and in September 1874, just prior to the expiration of the time allowed them in which to subscribe, they resolved not to avail themselves of the privilege. It was evident however, that the Company were favourably impressed with the bridge scheme, at one time wishing to subscribe and obtaining running powers, but to the exclusion of the Midland Railway – an arrangement which was found to be impossible.

It will be noticed that the original design contemplated a footway over the bridge and as this would be of great convenience to the public, an application was made to the county authorities to guarantee the cost of construction and maintenance and, in support of the application, it was urged that the tolls would, if not immediately, at least ultimately, meet such expense. The Court of Quarter Sessions appointed a committee to confer with the directors of the Severn Bridge Railway Company on the subject. It was estimated that the cost of the footway would be £10,000 and the Severn Bridge Railway offered to construct this amenity for that sum provided the county gave a guarantee that the tolls received by the company should represent five per cent on the outlay, and £150 for repairs and maintenance, the County to fix the tolls, which were to be not less than a penny-halfpenny for each person.

The committee reported against the proposition and in their report said 'Considering that large facilities must be afforded by the railway company for short passenger trains crossing the river when the bridge is constructed, and a station for passengers opened, as is represented to be intended at each end of the bridge, and that no reliable information is obtainable as to the probable traffic under the present state of the population, should such facilities for crossing the river be afforded, the amount of traffic to be anticipated in future when the docks are opened and trade developed, must be conjecture. Much difference of opinion existed among the members of the committee as to the prudence of making the ratepayers of the county responsible for securing so large a sum as £650 per annum as tolls to be collected from foot passengers crossing the river and it was determined by a small majority to report to the County Quarter Sessions that in the opinion of this committee, it is not expedient to accept the offer of the company made to the last Quarter Sessions.'

At a meeting at the *Canal Office*, Gloucester, in August 1874, G.W. Keeling presented the engineer's report and it was learned that work was proceeding in preparing the bridge drawings and surveying. He stated that in accordance with the survey and the working drawings, the present position was as follows. The centre line had been staked out on the land and the working longitudinal and cross-sections taken. The whole of the land plans were complete and placed in the hands of the Company's solicitor. The drawings of the swing bridge over the canal extensions were finished, but the working drawings of the Severn Bridge required great consideration to detail and therefore could not be hurried, but they hoped to be in the position to complete the drawings of that portion of the structure crossing the river, within two months from that date.

1874 has now slipped quietly past and in February 1875, at the half-yearly meeting[1] of the Severn Bridge Railway Company, held at the Canal Offices, Gloucester, W.C. Lucy presented the directors' report that they, the directors submitted statements of the Company's accounts for the half year ending 31 December 1874, prepared in the form required by the Regulation of Railways Act of 1868. Since the last meeting the Severn & Wye Railway and Canal Company had nominated J. Grahame Clarke as their representative. The directors of the Great Western Railway Company had declined to take the shares reserved for them.

At the same meeting, the engineer's report was presented by Keeling and Wells Owen who said they had the pleasure of reporting on the previous August that they had proceeded with the working drawings of the Severn Bridge Railway and had completed those for the bridge crossing the river and the railway on the Lydney side in November. The detail drawings for the swing bridge over the Gloucester and Berkeley Canal and for the railway on the Berkeley side of the river were nearing completion.

The specifications and bills of quantities for the contracts were prepared and invitations to tender issued on 15 December last. The Board of Trade and the engineer of the Severn Commission had approved the design and position of the piers of the bridge in the river. The Board of Trade had also conveyed to the Company their rights in the bed of the river and foreshore.

The Contractors

Prior to the commencement of the contract, S.H. Loutitt and Samuel

Sharrock, civil engineer and manager for Hamiltons Windsor Iron Works Company had stood on the bank at Purton for the first time, looking at the swirling water below, and then up at a black and white striped pole which had been erected, representing the full height of the bridge at that point, Loutitt enquired of Sharrock whether he was prepared to carry out the work, to which Sharrock replied in the affirmative. Loutitt then enquired whom he should employ as the bridge manager, to which Sharrock replied that he would appoint George Earle who had worked for the Company for over ten years, during which time he had erected most difficult structures.

The contract for the bridge was won by Hamiltons Windsor Iron Works Company Limited of London and Garston, Liverpool; and this involved the erection and founding of the pier cylinders through the river bed, erecting and rivetting twenty-one Parabolic or Bow String spans and the swing bridge over the canal, and the erection of the North Docks Branch swing bridge adjacent to the New Docks.

To Messrs. Vickers & Cooke of London fell the task of erecting the North Docks Branch viaduct, masonry piers for both swing bridges, Sharpness abutments and pier No. 1 near the old canal; Purton viaduct and Severn Bridge Tunnel, 506 yards long, under line bridges, cuttings and stations.

The Laying of the Foundation Stone

At long last the Severn Bridge Railway project began to gather momentum; almost three years had passed since the Bill received Royal Assent, when on Thursday 3 July 1875, in a quiet unostentatious manner, the first stone was laid of the Severn Bridge.[2] No public ceremony was expected when the officials concerned arrived at the site, but they soon found that preparations had been made in the form of a local gathering who had assembled on the foreshore at Purton. The official party were met at the site by Lucy and Keeling, the occasion having been preceded by an office meeting.

The stone, two tons in weight, had been previously prepared. At precisely 2.00p.m. the Directors made their appearance, the site for the ceremony having been previously fenced off near the bank of the river. Those present were: W.C. Lucy, chairman; W.B. Clegram, vice chairman; J.A. Grahame Clarke, chairman, Severn & Wye Railway and Canal Company; G.B. Keeling, secretary, Severn & Wye Railway and Canal Company; G.B. LLoyd, Midland Railway, H. Loutitt, Hamiltons Windsor Iron Works Company; Mr. Cooke, Vickers & Cooke; G.W. Keeling and G. Wells Owen, engineers, H. Waddy, secretary, Sharpness Dock

Company; Messrs. Wilton and Riddiford, solicitors to the Severn Bridge Railway Company, W. Nicks, C. Walker, H.M. James, T.N. Foster and G. Richards, secretary, Severn Bridge Railway and O. Reichenbach, assistant engineer.

The two ton block was laid on solid rock by W.C. Lucy, who mounted the block and briefly addressed those assembled. He remarked that on the previous day he had had no knowledge that he would be called upon to perform the ceremony or take part in the proceedings and it was to his great pleasure to find so much interest being shown in the undertaking, so long after the Act. He was pleased that the first practical step had been taken and he knew so many present were aware of the great difficulties which had now been overcome. He then quoted from Shakespeare, 'Now is the winter of our discontent, made glorious summer by this sun of York, And all the clouds that lowered upon our house. . . .' adding in his own words 'lie in the Severn buried'. He concluded by declaring the foundation stone well and truly laid.

Three cheers were given for the Severn Bridge and three for the directors. The party then repaired to the engineers' rooms (at Purton Manor) and partook of lunch. Later a special train placed at their disposal transported the directors to Gloucester.

At the Purton Passage Inn (Now Severn Bridge Hotel) a large number of people assembled during the evening and Mr. Godfrey, the landlord provided a brass band for the evening's entertainment.

At the half-yearly meeting[3] held in August, Keeling and Owen presented the engineer's report, this was to the effect that Hamiltons Windsor Iron Works Company were pushing forward the work at their establishment at Garston. They had cast nearly 100 pier cylinders, six feet in diameter, and a similar number of cast iron cross bracings that joined the cylinders together, some of the nine and ten feet pier cylinders had also been cast. The castings and wrought iron superstructure of the swing bridge was in hand, and work had commenced on the wrought iron work of the 134 foot spans.

At the site of the bridge at Sharpness, workshops had been built, scows and barges constructed and the necessary plant provided. The piles for the stagings of two of the piers in the river had been driven and about fifty cylinders delivered. The sinking of the cylinders would commence immediately.

Messrs. Vickers and Cooke during the previous April received orders to commence the viaduct across the dock lands at Sharpness, the swing bridge over the canal and the masonry abutments of the bridge on the west shore. Subsequently on 2 July, they were placed in possession of the whole of the land required for the approaches on the Lydney side.

Lydbrook Viaduct in its early stages of construction; this was George Keeling's first major civil engineering project, and he was presented with a silver salver on its completion

Author's Collection

Purton Manor, the home of the engineers during construction; the Manor was reputed to have been the home of Sir Walter Raleigh.

Author's Collection

The dock viaduct was progressing and the deep cutting near Purton had been commenced and part of the fencing erected.

The construction of the Severn Bridge was an immense project in its day and one which presented the engineers with numerous but not insuperable problems, and the tidal influence of the Severn and the roaring south-westerly gales that lashed the estuary, added their contribution to the hazards of the project. The spring tides of the river rose to a height of thirty to thirty-four feet at speeds of eight to ten knots, dependent on the direction and velocity of the wind; and where the bridge crossed the deep navigation channel to Wheel Rock, huge eddies and vortexes caused many anxious moments.

At Purton Manor, near the bridge site, on the west bank, Keeling, Wells Owen and their assistant and resident engineer O. Reichenbach, obtained rooms as their headquarters throughout the project and nearby a footbridge was erected over the South Wales line, for easy access to the shore.

At Sharpness, on the inland bank of the canal, adjacent to the junction of the old and new docks, a large contractors' yard was established equipped with workshops, a railway branch and facilities for boat building.

The cylinders for the piers were cast and the spans fabricated and erected at Garston, finally dismantled, and shipped to Sharpness in numbered sections and later shipped to the contractors site for final erection.

1876   The Engineers' Progress Report

At a meeting[4] at the Canal Office, Gloucester on 5 February, Keeling and Owen reported on the work of the past half year. They said that progress by Hamiltons Windsor Iron Works Company was satisfactory and that the mode of executing the work and the quality of materials was in accordance with the contract. The sinking of the pier cylinders had commenced on 15 August and the cylinders of eleven of the piers had been sunk through twenty-eight feet of sand to rock. The air compressing apparatus was now complete and the operation of founding the cylinders into rock and filling them with concrete would shortly commence. The scaffolding for the erection of the first two spans was almost ready and seven spans 134 feet long had been delivered to the site at Sharpness and were ready for erection. The swing bridge structure for crossing the new canal was also delivered. Two of the 174 foot spans were erected at the works at Garston and the remainder of the small spans were in progress. Cast iron for the cylinders delivered

2nd May 1876. A Sisson & White pile driving engine mounted on a scow drives the piles for Pier No. 15.

8th May 1876. 10 foot diameter pier cylinders standing in the contractors yard, while George Keeling poses for his photograph.

including those erected amounted to 780 tons, and wrought iron delivered about 780 tons. The work on the railway approaches was proceeding, the earthworks on the Lydney side amounted to 30,000 cubic yards and on the Sharpness side, part of the viaduct across the docklands had been erected and fencing was nearly completed throughout.

At the same meeting, Lucy announced that the Severn Bridge and Bristol Port and Channel Dock Junction Railway Bill had been withdrawn, but the directors were watching the progress of the Severn Bridge and Forest of Dean Central Railway Bill.[5]

This Bill was intended to link the Severn Bridge Railway with the Forest of Dean Central Railway by a branch which left the Severn Bridge near Purton Viaduct via Lower Etloe, passing near Oatfield Farm and joining the Forest of Dean Central Railway at Hagloe Park, another branch from the Central at Blackpool Bridge completed a link with the Forest of Dean Branch of the Great Western Railway near the tunnel on the outskirts of Soudley.

Although the plans were deposited with the Clerk of the Peace at Gloucester, the scheme was eventually abandoned.

An early set back

The engineer's plan was to commence construction on the east bank across a high sand bank called 'The Ridge'. During the neap tide period, the Ridge was covered by only a few feet of water and progress was expected to be fairly rapid.

It was at this stage that the first problem was encountered. The Ridge consisted of a mixture of sand with a high percentage of clay, approximately thirty feet deep. Great difficulty was experienced in driving the piles for the pier supports, which in effect, was likened to driving a bar into a block of rubber. Such slow progress was made, that an alternative method was sought.

James Brunlees, an engineer employed in the construction of a viaduct over the sands of Morecambe Bay, had encountered a similar problem where the sustaining power of the sand was approximately five tons per square foot. His answer to the problem was to design a hydraulic pile[6] consisting of a hollow iron tube, nine feet long and ten inches outer diameter by three-quarters of an inch thick, with a thirty inch diameter disc or plate at the base. In the centre of the disc was a two inch diameter orifice for discharging water. The piles were sunk from a pontoon fitted with a pile engine and a donkey engine of approximately two horse power. The piles were lashed to the block of the pile engine which acted as a guide, with another guide low down on the pontoon, the pile hanging with a loose chain, so that its weight assisted in the sinking. An attachment was made with a flexible hose to the donkey engine and water was pumped in at the top of the pile and on issuing at the orifice scoured away the sand. Removing the piles was accomplished by pumping and lifting with the pile engine.

Brunlee's method, though slightly modified, was adopted with great success on the Severn Bridge. The piles in this case being of timber, it was decided to fit a pipe extending down the entire length of the pile, and on pumping water down the pipe, it was found that very little force was required to drive the pile home. The staging for stabilising the piers was then erected in a box form with timber guides for maintaining the piers in a vertical position. A method was devised utilising a system of screws and links enabling the pier cylinders to be added at the top of the staging. A coating of red lead applied to the machined faces of the cylinders was sufficient to render them water tight.

When the piers had been lowered onto the bed rock and built up to a safe height above high water, the next phase of the operation was the hazardous work of founding the piers into the rock. To accomplish this, the accumulation of sand had to be first excavated from the interior of the pier. The top section of the pier was fitted with a large iron air bell with a projecting compartment containing an air lock, and a winch in the air bell, externally operated, provided hoisting facilities for removing the accumulation of sand and rock from the foundations. A steam driven air compressor supplied air to the pier via the air bell and to counterbalance the buoyant effect created by the compressed air, sections of rail were suspended from the sides of the pier. During the early stages of construction, the air pressure supplied to the pier was fairly low, but when founding the deep water piers, the pressure was raised considerably and ballast weights increased to over one hundred tons, bearing in mind that the deepest foundation was seventy feet below high water at the spring tides.

On extracting the sand, the rock bed of the river was excavated to a depth of four feet with Reeves pneumatic excavators, a tedious task in the confined space of the cylinders only nine feet and ten feet in diameter. For many years the older inhabitants of the locality recalled how the workmen emerged from the air lock in an exhausted condition bleeding from the ears and noses.

As the excavating proceeded, the whole pier assembly was inched down into the excavation and the foundation was filled with concrete and the air pressure maintained until it had set, finally the air bell was removed.

The remaining pier cylinders above the foundations were lined with felt to cater for expansion and contraction and topped up with concrete and a large stone weighing five to six tons was placed on the top most cylinder and remained until the concrete had set.

Erection of the 134 foot spans

With the piers safely founded, the staging was continued up to almost the full height of the bridge and an additional support erected at the centre of the span to support the longitudinal members of the staging, which were also fitted with rails to accommodate a travelling crane which traversed the full length of the span. The permanent way decking was then laid out on packing pieces and the horizontal trusses composed of laminations hoisted into position, followed by the vertical bracings and finally the inner and outer plates of the top chordal trusses and diagonals; the whole assembly being bolted together as a temporary measure prior to rivetting. Walkways and trestling for access to the top trusses were installed and hand operated forges provided heat for the rivets. The rivetting was carried out by blacksmiths, each rivet being set by hand and inspected after setting. In spite of the work involved, many of the 134 foot spans were erected in a week prior to rivetting and later Clegram complimented the contractors on their efficient handling of the project.

It will be noticed that the pier cylinders had, at this stage, only been erected to a safe height above high water; the mid-span staging was then utilized as a platform to install a winch with which to hoist the remaining pier cylinders into position; later, steam driven winches were installed to speed up the operations. The remaining cylinders were bolted together by workmen, working from ladders inside the cylinders, which were eventually lined and filled with concrete.

The pier section immediately below the top most cylinder was of a variable length, machined to order to maintain the datum throughout the length of the bridge, bearing in mind the bridge was built on an incline, which terminated at the summit in the middle of the Severn Bridge Tunnel at Purton.

On completing the piers, the fixed roller bearing and movable rocker bearing were fitted and the span lowered, by removing the packing pieces. The piers were finally drilled and tapped and the lattice cross bracings fitted, the ornamental finials capping the piers erected and the assembly was ready for painting.

3rd July 1876. The staging is erected for the masonry viaduct at Purton; dirty work on the banks of the river, note the trousers hanging out to dry on the staging.

Author's Collection

George Earle, manager of the bridge project, surveys the scene from two partially erected pier cylinders.

Author's Collection

14th November 1876. The Contractors yard now well established along the bank of the Gloucester & Berkeley Canal.

Cylinders for Pier No. 14 being sunk; the group of men on the left are operating an air pump for supplying divers bolting up the sections.

Trouble in the Severn & Wye Company

The Severn and Wye Railway and Canal Company were now lamenting at the depression of the trade in the Forest, primarily from strikes and the unsettled state of the labour market, and at their meeting at the Royal Hotel, Bristol, H. Roper, a shareholder, rose to champion the cause of his unfortunate colleagues. He stated that their unfortunate railway was paying the shareholders a handsome dividend a few years ago, but it was now reduced to the state that the ordinary shareholder had not received one penny for the last three-and-a-half years, but preference shareholders were still receiving four-and-a-half percent and some, two percent. Other shareholders were also bickering at the Company's subscription to the Severn Bridge, while Grahame Clark, the chairman urged the need for rigid economy as the Company's receipts had fallen to a low and dangerous level.

The doubling of the swing bridge

Early in February, a special meeting was held, the main item on the agenda being the question of constructing the swing bridge for a double track. Clegram presided in the absence of Lucy. He said he would like to make a few remarks regarding the progress of the bridge. He thought the engineers had been very modest in their progress reports. As engineer at Sharpness, he had had constant opportunities of watching the work in progress and this could only be characterised as rapid. He had rarely seen work carried out with so much system as that of the bridge and the shareholders might congratulate themselves that the work was in the hands of contractors who were likely to carry it out successfully.

With regard to the approaches, he thought this work was not proceeding as satisfactorily as it should, but he believed the engineers were satisfied that the work was now proceeding more rapidly and would be ready as soon as the bridge was completed. On the question of the swing bridge, he thought it would be unwise to construct it in such a manner as to make it difficult to construct the whole of the railway for a double track. The original estimated cost for the swing bridge was £15,000 and the cost of the doubling of the line at this point would not exceed £10,000. He said that Lucy and himself had conferred with T.E. Harrison, the consultant engineer, who was strongly in favour of doubling the swing bridge, and that if this question was left until the bridge was open, the stoppage of traffic would be nothing short of disastrous. He also pointed out that the block system diminished the traffic by at least half, and there would be occasional delays owing to the passage of vessels on the canal, and he had strongly advised them to proceed with the necessary alterations.

Clegram said he was wholly in favour of this action being taken, the resolution was moved and all the directors voted in favour.

A special meeting was called on 7 February and the directors were informed that a Bill[7] for confirming additional powers on the Severn Bridge Railway Company had been applied for, the object of which was to raise additional capital for widening the swing bridge, additional protection to the piers in the channel, and for the provision of stations, rails and signals.

The Bill also applied for additional time for the completion of the project and one very important clause provided for a guarantee of interest on borrowed capital to an amount not exceeding £75,000 subscribed jointly by the Midland Railway Company, Sharpness New Docks and the Gloucester and Birmingham Navigation Company, which would enable the Company to borrow at a lower rate of interest than they could have done simply on the security of the Company itself.

Lucy remarked that those who had recently read of the Tay Bridge disaster might naturally feel a little anxious as to the Severn Bridge, but it would be satisfactory to the shareholders to know that during the recent heavy gales — gales unprecedented of late years — no part of the structure had given way in the slightest. Nine spans had been completed, extending over one third of the way across the river. Lucy was asked by a shareholder if he would like to venture a statement as to a time when the bridge would be completed, to which he replied that in such an undertaking as was in hand, it was always doubtful but he believed the railway would open two years hence.

The engineers' report

At the half-yearly meeting[8] at the Canal Office on 21 February, Lucy told the directors and shareholders that the cost of the additional work had rendered a further outlay of capital for the completion of the undertaking and the Bill for this purpose would sanction the raising of an additional share capital of £100,000. Keeling and Wells Owen reported that Hamiltons Windsor Iron Works Company had continued to make satisfactory progress in spite of the unfavourable weather of the winter. The cylinders for twelve piers had been founded and filled with concrete, three other piers were in progress and ten had been built up to full height and were complete to the underside of the spans. Five spans were erected and completely rivetted and four more in various stags of erection. The swing bridge over the new canal had been completed and iron work for the swing bridge over the old canal was being delivered. The circular masonry pier to carry the swing bridge was well advanced

10th September 1877. George Keeling (seventh from the left) visits the contractors yard at Garston, Liverpool. The first 312 foot span stands in the background.

Author's Collection

15th May 1877. Severn Bridge Tunnel, 506 yards long, being opened up to its full size. The scene of one of the first fatalities on the project.

Author's Collection

41

1st August 1877. The air bell with its air lock seen in use founding the piers. The blowing engine is on the left.

and constructional difficulties had been overcome, and the foundations of masonry pier no. 1 were almost complete. Cast iron for cylinders, machinery etc., delivered was 2,800 tons and wrought iron delivered was 2,400 tons. The work of the other contractors had not been so satisfactory but the total earthworks completed was approximately 116,000 cubic yards. Two piers of the masonry viaduct at Purton had been commenced and the heading for the tunnel driven throughout.

The amalgamation

On Tuesday 29 April 1878, the Severn & Wye Railway and Canal Company, and Severn Bridge Railway Company Amalgamation Bill[9] came before the Select Committee of the House of Commons. Mr. Backhouse presided with Mr. Granville Somerset Q.C., and Mr. Dugdale representing the promoters, Mr. Round Q.C., and Mr. Saunders appeared to oppose the Bill on behalf of the Great Western Railway.

Granville Somerset in opening the case for the promoters said that the two railways were very small and the amalgamation was desirable for economy and in the public interest. The Severn Bridge line was very short and was placed between two powerful companies and on this ground it was desirable that the amalgamation should take place.

The first witness W.C. Lucy, described the Act under which the Severn Bridge Railway Company was formed and expressed the opinion that the amalgamation would be of great service to the two companies he represented.

Mr. Potter, a director of the Severn Bridge Railway, and a former chairman of the Great Western Railway, also largely connected with several other railways said he believed the amalgamation would be beneficial, generally, by strengthening the two companies and thus preventing them being absorbed by some larger company, which would, if it could monopolise the traffic of the district.

J.A. Grahame Clarke, chairman of the Severn & Wye Railway and Canal Company entirely concurred with Lucy's and Potter's evidence, and other witnesses called in support of the promoters case were, G.B. Keeling, general manager of the Severn & Wye Railway and Canal Company, W.B. Clegram, G.W. Keeling, T.F. Brown, deputy gaveller of the Forest of Dean also representing the Crown in respect of mineral properties, and W.B. Brain of Trafalgar Colliery.

Henry Tennant, general manager of the North Eastern Railway Company was also called. He said the North Eastern Railway Company consisted of thirty-three amalgamations and therefore he had much experience to offer on the subject. He thought the two companies were too small to live apart and sooner or later the only solution would be amalgamation. In this case it was a perfectly natural alliance.

This concluded the case for the promoters and Round, on behalf of the Great Western Railway Company opposed the preamble on the grounds that it had not been shown that any advantage to the public would accrue from the proposed amalgamation and pointed out that the application was premature inasmuch as the railway was not yet completed.

The committee found the preamble proved, and the Bill received Royal Assent 21 July 1878.

The two companies entered into negotiations on the question of amalgamation which resulted in their agreeing to this on the following terms: That for the first two years after the opening of the Severn Bridge Railway to traffic, the net receipt of the two companies should be apportioned seventy per cent to the Severn & Wye and thirty per cent to the Severn Bridge Railway, for the third fifty-five per cent to the Severn & Wye and forty-five per cent to the Severn Bridge Railway and subsequently fifty per cent to each company, and the two companies to be known as the Severn & Wye Section and the Bridge Section, the undertaking to be known as the Severn & Wye and Severn Bridge Railway on the opening of the railway.

The hazards of the channel

The contractors had now reached the most critical phase in the construction of the bridge, that of crossing the navigation channel. The first attempts in the erection of the staging, met with early failure when the staging was washed away by the tides and some partly erected cylinders had to be recovered ready for the second attempt. The staging timbers were now very substantial, the base consisting of three rows of piles each fifteen inches square driven by a Sisson and White pile driver. The base of the staging was cross braced from top to bottom and fitted with cut water dolphins, as an added precaution against collision by shipping.

The necessity for the more massive staging would be apparent if a few facts were mentioned concerning the force of the tides in this particular area. On one occasion, the staging was being dismantled, and on reaching the base piles and having removed the cross bracings between the three rows, the work was abandoned owing to the imminent turn of the tide; later it was found that all the piles had been snapped off at river bed level leaving only the stumps. On another occasion two large stones weighing five to six tons for placing on top of the piers, were left on the lower staging eight feet above the low water line. There was a high tide that night and next morning the stones had disappeared from sight. The workmen were so astonished that some doubted that the stones had ever been placed there, but the doubts were dispelled when the stones were located sixty feet away.

The engineers' report 3 August 1878

'During the past six months the Hamiltons Windsor Iron Company have successfully overcome the difficulties in founding the deep water piers No. 19 and No. 20, both of these piers being composed of a group of four cylinders ten feet in diameter. They are situated in the channel of the river and are exposed to the greatest force of the tidal currents, the depth at high water to the bottom of the foundations being seventy-five feet. Pier No. 19 has been founded in rock and built up to full height, three of the cylinders of pier No. 20 are founded in rock and the fourth is now in progress. Pier 21 has been built up to full height and all piers are complete with the exception of No. 20. The five 174 foot spans have been erected, making eighteen spans of the bridge complete. There remains to be erected one 134 foot span and two 312 foot spans, the scaffolding for one of the latter is now in the course of erection. The iron work for the swing bridge across the old canal, is now completed and the engines, boilers and machinery for turning it, is now being installed.

The work on the railway approaches formerly included in the contract of Messrs. Vickers and Cooke is now being carried out by Griffith Griffiths of Lydney who are making good progress. Two miles of the line has been completed on the Lydney side and the cuttings at both ends of the tunnel are nearly finished. Fifty yards of the tunnel (506 yards long) remain to be excavated and lined and will probably be completed by September next. The largest amount of work remaining to be executed is about 2,000 cubic yards of masonry in the viaduct at Purton and 100,000 cubic yards of earthwork on the Sharpness side.[10]

The end in sight

It was noted that the Vickers and Cooke contract was now in the hands of a local man Griffith Griffiths. For two years, the work on the approaches had lagged behind, finally almost to a standstill. An ultimatum was issued to the firm and eventually the contract was handed to Griffiths, but much remained to be done.

The erection of the 174 foot spans had proceeded steadily after the earlier setbacks and the end was now in sight with only three spans remaining to be erected. Hamiltons Windsor Iron Works Company now switched operations to the west bank were part of the viaduct was complete and the last span of 134 feet was erected.

Some difficulty had once again been experienced in the erection of the last three piers, the depth of water at this point being so great that higher pressures were necessary inside the cylinders to render them watertight; this in turn meant additional ballast weights being hung round the piers to counteract any buoyant effects and to stabilise the piers against the early rush of the tides, thus giving a greater margin of safety to those working seventy feet below high water.

During this phase of construction, one of the workmen fell over seventy feet to the base on to rock, with the very high air pressure in the cylinders his fall was cushioned and the only injury received was a broken arm.

The erection of the staging for the first of the 312 foot spans between piers 20 and 21 presented no further problems and once more the staging was of massive construction to take the weight of the immense horizontal trusses. This was the most critical point in the erection of the large spans, the safe stage in erection would only be reached when the top chordal trusses were safely in position and rivetted. The failure of the staging in the early stages of erection would mean the loss of valuable materials and time.

Fortunately, the work proceeded without mishap and by the end of the year, the erection of the first 312 foot span was well under way. It was completed in February 1879, an event which brought a sigh of relief from the engineers.

By May 1879, work on the last 312 foot span was falling behind schedule and to the rescue came Francis William Thomas Brain,[11] consulting engineer to the Electric Blasting Apparatus Company of Cinderford. He installed a system of floodlighting on the bridge, powered by a 'Gramme machine', thus enabling a night shift to be employed on the bridge. It is believed that Brain's system was later used for a floodlit football match in the Forest, not a new innovation as floodlit football had previously taken place on the Spa Ground at Gloucester in 1877.

Brain was born in 1855 and became an Associate Member of the Institute of Civil Engineers and later was knighted when President of the Colliery Owners Association. In 1882, he installed the first underground electrically driven pumps at Trafalgar Colliery.

The last span was completed in August and during the same month the contractors commenced laying the permanent way. The original track was laid on longitudinal timbers and was composed of sixty-five pounds Rhymney steel, hollow crown running rails and forty-eight pounds 'L' section guard rails as stipulated by the Board of Trade for bridges of this type. This type of track remained on the bridge until 1932, when it was relaid, the 'L' section guard rails being scrapped and replaced with eighty-five pound rails, similar rails also being used for running.

The base of the piers up to the high water mark was painted black, the remainder chocolate, with the spans finished in cream, and by early September, the whole of the railway was completed.

On 3 and 4 October the process of load testing the Severn Bridge began under the direction of Colonel F.A. Rich, R.E., Board of Trade Inspector, assisted by Keeling, Earle and Reichenbach.

Eight locomotives were involved in the tests consisting of rolling and static loads applied to each span, the rolling being conducted at a variety of speeds. The deflection of the 312 foot spans was noted as one and a half inches.

Sharpness Swing Bridge pier nearing completion. A Clayton & Shuttleworth lime mill driven by a Burrell portable steam engine was used in the manufacture of mortar or cement.

Author's Collection

The trow 'Victoria' registered at Chepstow unloads barrels of cement for filling the piers; The 'Victoria' was later wrecked on the bridge. Note the ballast weights hung around the left-hand pier to overcome the buoyant effect of the compressed air.

Author's Collection

Although the formal opening of the Severn Bridge did not take place for another month, the first train to carry passengers ran over the full length of the railway from Lydney to Sharpness on Wednesday 3 September 1879.[12] The trip was of a private nature and no preparations were made to celebrate the event. Among the party were W.C. Lucy, S.S. Marling, M.P., Captain Price, M.P., Major Bourne, C.B. Walker, W. Nicks, C. Sturge, J.M. Sturge, Mr. Pastons, W.B. Clegram, G.W. Keeling, H. Waddy, George Earle, contract manager; Griffith Griffiths, contractor, W.F. Hobrough, engineer Worcester & Birmingham Canal Company, Mr. George, local agent to Worcester & Birmingham Canal Company and Mr. Stalvies, Gloucester station master.

The party departed from Gloucester by the 11.15a.m. train to Lydney and travelled in a luxurious saloon carriage placed at their disposal by the Great Western Railway Company. On arrival at Lydney the carriage was detached from the train and shunted onto the Severn Bridge line, where a Severn & Wye locomotive was coupled for the journey to Sharpness. On arrival at Sharpness the directors of the Canal Company proceeded to the chairman's office where a meeting had been arranged to transact the Company's business, while the remainder of the party, not involved, roamed the New Docks. At 2.30p.m. the party assembled on the Canal Company's steamer *Sabrina* for luncheon and later proceeded to Sharpness Station on foot to rejoin their special train.

Proceeding to the bridge the train then stopped and the passengers alighted to inspect the bridge; at this point the party separated, some returning to Gloucester via the canal on *Sabrina* and the remainder to Lydney by train. At Lydney, congratulations were expressed at the successful conclusion of the undertaking and thanks to those who had kindly made the necessary arrangements for an event of such importance in local history, as the first train over the Severn Bridge.

No reference was made to the driver and locomotive which had hauled its passengers over the bridge. In all probability, the driver was William Ridler of Lydney and the locomotive *Maid Marion*. Ridler at the time was the chief driver of the Severn & Wye Railway and *Maid Marion* was considered the top locomotive of the Company and normally driven by Ridler.

H.W. Paar's *Severn & Wye Railway* refers to the colourful character of Ridler who found himself in disgrace on more than one occasion, due to his fondness for 'a glass'.

Bridge load tests on the London and North Western Railway – similar methods were used by Colonel Rich in load testing the Severn Bridge.

Author's Collection

A group of workmen pose on Wheel Rock, *c.* August 1879. Keeling is seen in the centre.

Author's Collection

An old milestone near Yorkley gives the distance to Purton Passage Ferry.

R. Huxley

Presentation to George Earle

A presentation was held at the Severn Bridge Railway Company's Office on 15 October when George Earle, the manager of Hamiltons Windsor Iron Works Company, was presented with a large gold hunting watch by the directors of the Severn Bridge Railway Company, the case of the watch being inscribed with the following:— 'Presented to George Earle, by the Directors of the Severn Bridge Railway Company in recognition of his zeal and ability and uniform cheerfulness in carrying out the works of the Severn Bridge, under exceptional difficulties for the Hamiltons Windsor Iron Works Co.'

The watch was supplied by W.C. Mann of Gloucester.

Clegram paid a glowing tribute to Earle. He said that on numerous occasions he had seen Earle confronted with immense problems which at times, were as much as he could bear, but the cheerful way in which he approached them and the way he handled his men in hazardous and difficult conditions, especially when founding and erecting the pier cylinders, earned him the respect of everyone connected with the project. Both Hamiltons Windsor Iron Works Company and the Severn

Bridge Railway Company were most fortunate in obtaining the services of a man of the calibre of George Earle.

The scene was now set for the final act, the opening of the new railway.

For several weekends, the bridge was thrown open for public inspection when special permits were issued by Earle at Purton Manor, and Keeling at Lydney, and on the last weekend prior to the opening day, which had been finalised as 17 October, over 1,000 people walked across the bridge, at last the east and west banks of the Severn were united. It was also announced that a banquet would be held at the Pleasure Grounds, Sharpness, to those familiar with the locality the site of the banquet was in recent years occupied by the Merchant Navy Training Establishment *Vindicatrix* where many of today's merchant seamen completed their initial training and were later 'outward bound' from Sharpness.

Fatalities on the Severn Bridge

Throughout the years, great civil engineering projects, such as bridges and tunnels had claimed the lives of those who pioneered the great railway systems we have today, and the Severn Bridge was no exception.

Today we are considered to be more safety conscious than in the Victorian era, but in spite of modern methods and machinery and safety precautions, there is an alarming toll in human lives in the construction of our new type of bridges, and naturally some credit must be given to those in charge of the Severn Bridge project, that in spite of the very primitive methods employed in its construction, only three fatalities took place on the whole of the railway, and only during the latter stages of the project.

On 8 January 1878 the first fatality occurred in the Severn Bridge Tunnel at Purton, when John Tomkins of Ruardean was killed while centre fixing. The inquest on the deceased was held at the Albert Inn, Lydney and evidence was given by John Parsons of Viney Hill and Mr. Kirby, a Foreman for Vickers and Cooke. Parsons told the Coroner and jury how a section of timber, approximately a ton in weight, had fallen on Tomkins when a rope securing it had slipped. M.F. Carter, the Forest of Dean Coroner returned a verdict of 'Accidental Death' and severely reprimanded Kirby for his lack of attention to safety and supervision.

Death rides the viaduct

Over a year passed before disaster struck again on Wednesday 1 March, when William Aston, aged sixty-four, of Lydney was killed in a fall while working on the viaduct at Purton.

At the inquest at Lydney Police Court, evidence was given by Stephen Morse, who stated that he resided at Purton and was an under-contractor in the masonry department constructing the viaduct. Aston and a youth named Drew operated the 'Traveller' (a travelling crane, for conveying stone blocks from one part of the viaduct to another). The Traveller moved on rails and had flanged wheels and the duties of Aston and Drew consisted on hoisting the stone blocks and working two handles with a pumping motion to propel the Traveller, and on 1 March were thus engaged, prior to the accident.

The Traveller had started from the centre of the viaduct towards No. 2 Arch near the bridge and was carrying a very large stone, when a heavy gust of wind blew up for about ten minutes. The Traveller was caught by the wind and ran on until it came to the end of the viaduct when it crashed into some timber staging at No. 1 Arch, where it was thrown off the rails and fell seventy feet to the ground. Aston fell twenty-five feet on to the staging and Drew escaped. On reaching Aston, he was found to be seriously injured and was removed to Severn Bridge station where he died at 1.40 in the afternoon.

Keeling was called and he told the jury that the Traveller was spragged when stationary, but had no brakes to slow it down when in motion, the only method of slowing the machine was by the handles that propelled it and this had proved adequate during normal conditions.

The Coroner, M.F. Carter, returned a verdict of 'Accidental Death'.

A fatality on the bridge

As previously stated, the most hazardous operation was that of erecting the bridge piers and spans. For many years after the opening of the bridge, a rumour had circulated that a luckless workman was entombed in one of the piers of bridge while concrete was being poured into the cylinders, where his body remained.

During the course of research, an extensive study of the Gloucester Journal was carried out and no press reports could be found relating to this particular accident, which can now be dismissed as local mythology.

The end of the project was in sight, when on Saturday 3 June 1879, tragedy again struck, this time on the bridge, when Thomas Roberts of

Henry Inman, the last proprietor of the Purton Passage Ferry, seen high on the Severn Bridge tending the navigation lights.

Wilfred Jones

Viney Hill, engaged on the erection of the last 312 foot span, fell from the permanent way level into the river. On the way down, he struck the staging, but he was rescued inside five minutes by an alert boatman, who had witnessed his fall.

He was removed to the Engineer's rooms at Purton Manor and Mr. Webb, a Surgeon of Blakeney, was called, but Roberts died shortly after his arrival.

The verdict of 'Accidently Death' was recorded by the Forest of Dean Coroner.

Drama in the river

Three days after the Directors of the Severn Bridge Railway Company had made their historic trip over the bridge (6 September) a further accident occurred, but this time not connected with the construction work.

The accident ended in the death of Thomas Shaw of Gatcombe, the proprietor of a well known fishing business owned by members of the Shaw family for many years. On 6 September, Shaw had been in Kingroad with his brother William and Thomas Margrate to purchase an anchor, and was returning in his strongest boat with the tide, which at the time was running with considerable force. On reaching the bridge, an effort was made to run through No. 19 span. There was little wind and while the occupants were rowing the boat, it was caught by a huge eddy and turned broadside. Before evasive action could be taken, the boat was swept out of control into the timber staging around one of the piers and was cut in two.

The occupants hung on to the staging, but later, the timber supporting Shaw collapsed, possibly from the force of the collision and the unfortunate man was swept away by the rising tide. William Shaw and Margrate with great difficulty, climbed the staging to some ladders, by which means they were able to reach the permanent way level, arriving there, they crossed the bridge to the Sharpness side and proceeded to the contractors office near the old docks, where they were loaned a boat by which they recrossed the river to Gatcombe and reported the accident.

On the following morning Earle gave instructions to the Company's divers to search for the missing body believing it to be caught in the staging. This was carried out under the supervision of Mr. Wyatt, but the search proved to be unsuccessful. The body was later recovered on Monday 9 September by David Long of Framilode.

On Tuesday evening M.F. Carter held an inquest at the Sloop Inn,

Gatcombe (now known as Drake's House) with J. Philpotts, a chemist of Blakeney as foreman of the jury. The coroner terminated the proceedings by briefly addressing the jury and in referring to the contractors of the bridge, said they had done everything possible to prevent such accidents, warning lights had been placed on the structure and had been seen by the occupants of the boat, but all control of the boat had been lost.

The jury returned a verdict of 'accidental death'.

References to Chapter Three

1. *Gloucester Journal* 28 February 1875.
2. *Gloucester Journal* 5 July 1875.
3. *Gloucester Journal* 28 August 1875.
4. *Gloucester Journal* 12 February 1875.
5. Gloucestershire Records Office (engineering plans)   Q RUM 406.
6. *Molesworths Book of Engineering Formulæ* Hydraulic Piles James Brunlees p.128.
7. Severn Bridge Railways Act 40 and 41. Vic. C. 148. 2 August 1877.
8. *Gloucester Journal* 24 February 1877.
9. Severn & Wye & Severn Bridge Railways Act 42 and 43 Vic C. 163.
10. *Gloucester Journal* late Supplement 3 August 1878.
11. *The Industrial History of Dean* by Dr. Cyril Hart. *The Gloucester Journal* 'The Opening of the Severn Bridge' 18 October 1879.
12. *Gloucester Journal* 6 September 1879.

CHAPTER FOUR

Peace has its Victories

The inauguration of the Severn Bridge Railway

Favoured with fine weather, the ceremony of inauguration of the Severn Bridge Railway for public traffic was performed on Friday 17 October,[1] with great success. Elaborate and liberal provision had been made to give the affair a character adequate to its importance and it was long since the locality had witnessed a gathering so imposing. In the neighbourhood of Sharpness Docks and on both sides of the river, an air of festivity prevailed. The Midland Railway Company ran excursions from Gloucester and the Great Western Company conveyed large numbers of passengers from Gloucester to Lydney, at special cut rate fares. The inhabitants of the Forest swarmed by their hundreds to the locality of the bridge, and at Sharpness a fair was held in a field overlooking the docks. Ships berthed in the docks, displayed their bunting and on each side of the bridge, the approaches were decorated with the flags of foreign nations.

The guests invited by the Company, numbered between 300 and 400, and were conveyed from Gloucester in a special train consisting of twenty-three first class carriages, and free railway tickets were issued to all the holders of invitation cards. The special was scheduled to leave Gloucester at 11.00a.m., but was delayed by the late arrival of the normal service train to Bristol, which it was booked to follow, stopping at several intermediate stations. The train arrived at the east end of the bridge shortly before noon, and was welcomed by crowds of sightseers as it rolled onto the solid and graceful structure of the new bridge.

The train arrived at Lydney Junction, and before commencing the return journey, the driver and fireman on the locomotive were joined by W.C. Lucy, the Earl of Bathurst, the Earl of Ducie, F. Allport, G.W. Keeling and W.P. Price. At a given signal, the train proceeded to the bridge and on crossing, a fog signal was exploded on each of the twenty-one spans, a royal salute for the opening of the first major railway bridge over the River Severn.

After a brief halt at Sharpness, the train once again crossed the bridge to the Purton end, where a large number of passengers alighted and proceeded to the first 312 foot span where Lucy tightened the last bolt.

56

Having completed this minor task of practical engineering, he declared the bridge completed and open for traffic. After three cheers for the bridge, many of the passengers made their way to Sharpness Station on foot, and from there to the Pleasure Grounds, where a large marquee had been erected and a magnificent luncheon prepared for nearly 400 guests. The luncheon, or banquet – for such it was – did great credit to the hospitality of the hosts and to the caterer R. Fortt of Westgate Street, Gloucester.

The banquet

The chairman (W.C. Lucy) sat at the centre of a raised table with the Earl of Bathurst on his right and the Earl of Ducie on his left and Grace was said by the Reverend J.L. Stackhouse. Amongst the guests were many notable personalities including Sir Daniel Gooch, chairman of the Great Western Railway Company, James Allport, general manager, Midland Railway Company, representatives of the Monmouth, Taff Vale and Andover Railways, Worcester and Birmingham Canal Company and Gloucester & Berkeley Canal Company, The Severn Tunnel and Ross & Monmouth Railways, Gloucester Town Council, Chamber of Commerce, colliery proprietors and iron masters of the Forest of Dean and South Wales, and the mayors of Tewkesbury, Cheltenham, Newport, Worcester and Birmingham. Hamiltons Windsor Iron Works Company, was represented by H.D. Davis, A. Edwards, S. Sharrock, G. Earle, H. Loutitt and Griffith Griffiths, and Vice Consuls of Germany, Denmark, France, U.S.A. and the Netherlands were also in attendance.

After the luncheon, Lucy proposed the toast 'The Queen, the Prince and Princess of Wales and the rest of the Royal Family' and later a toast to the 'Houses of Parliament'. Earl Bathurst responded for the House of Lords and Colonel Kingscote, M.P. for the House of Commons, both men passing reference to the bridge over which they had recently walked.

Lucy said he had to propose the health of a nobleman who, by his position, was the most direct representative of Her Majesty – the Lord Lieutenant, the Earl of Ducie. The inhabitants of the county knew how admirably he performed the duties of his office and how much he was esteemed and respected as a private person. He assured the visitors, to whom his Lordship was not known, that Gloucestershire men were very proud of their Lord Lieutenant.

The Earl of Ducie in responding said, 'I can assure you that among the various functions which a Lord Lieutenant is called upon to discharge, there is none more gratifying that when he is invited to assist

An early postcard by stationer W. Smith-Charley of Blakeney shows the original running rails and 'L' section guard rails, this type of track remained until 1932.

Author's Collection

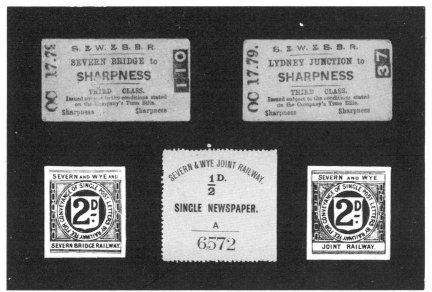

Tickets issued on the opening day found some years ago at Sharpness. Also railway letter stamps which ensured a quick delivery of items posted at your local station.

Author's Collection

in some great work which is for the benefit and is to the credit of the county in which he lives (Cheers). It has been my privilege today to cross the river by the bridge and also be brought back again in safety — no small matter. I have been placed in the very forefront of the battle, because the directors, doubtless animated by some sort of superstition, insisted upon my riding on the engine. As I went along, I had ample opportunity of noticing the airy span by which we travelled and the rushing river and treacherous sands below, and without any knowledge of engineering, it was impossible not to see that very great difficulties had been overcome by the science, skill and courage of those who had undertaken this great enterprise. At the same time, one cannot fail to see that capital must have been attracted to it and when I come to ask why, the answer is that it is because the gentleman who is at the head of this undertaking, is one in whom all his friends and neighbours have the utmost confidence (Cheers). They know he will not lend his hand to anything that is not upright and honourable, and has always acted forcibly in a gentle fashion to carry out this great enterprise to a successful issue. I have now to propose 'The Chairman and Directors of the Severn Bridge Railway'.

The chairman, having acknowledged the compliment said 'I can

WYE VALLEY LINE AND COLEFORD BRANCH.

Down Trains.		Week Days only.				Up Trains.		Week Days only.			
		a.m.	a.m.	p.m.	p.m.			a.m.	a.m.	p.m.	p.m.
Coleford .... dep	8 24	11 55	2 15	5 29		Bristol (Temple Meads) . dep	5 55	4	1 45	5 15		
Newland .... ,,	8 31	12 2	2 25	5 36		Severn Tunnel Junction ... ,,	6 55		2	6 17		
Monmouth (Troy) .... arr	8 45	12 16	2 45	5 50		Chepstow .... dep	7 13			6 00		
Monmouth (Troy) .... dep	9 0	12 35	4 0	6 0		Tidenham .... ,,	7 19	11 31	2 55	6 14		
Redbrook .... ,,	9 6	12 43	4 6	6 6		Tintern .... ,,	7 29	11 43	3 8	6 51		
Bigsweir .... ,,	9 14	12 51	4 14	6 14		Bigsweir .... ,,	7 36	11 49	3 15	6 58		
Tintern .... ,,	9 22	1 0	4 23	6 24		Redbrook .... ,,	7 43	11 47	3 22	7 5		
Tidenham .... ,,	9 30	1 8	4 31	6 32		Monmouth (Troy) ...... arr	7 50	11 53	3 29	7 12		
Chepstow .... arr	9 37	1 16	4 39	6 39		Monmouth (Troy) ...... dep	7 56	9 40	12	4 46		
Severn Tunnel Junction . arr	9 55	1 33	4 57	6 55		Newland .... ,,	8 12	9 54	1 11	5 5		
Bristol (Temple Meads) . ,,	11 2	2 47	7 0	7 53		Coleford .... arr	8 19	10 1		5 12		

SEVERN AND WYE AND SEVERN BRIDGE. (All Trains are 1st and 3rd class only)

Down Trains.		Week Days only.											
		a.m.	a.m.	a.m.	p.m.	p.m.	p.m.	p.m.	p.m.	p.m.	p.m.		
BERKELEY ROAD ...... dep		8 50	11 14		2 19		4 10		6 5		8 20		
Berkeley .... ,,		8 57	11 21		2 25		4 17		6 11		8 27		SATURDAYS ONLY
Sharpness .... ,,		9 3	11 27		2 31	3 45	4 23		6 17		8 33		
Severn Bridge (for Blakeney) ,,		9 8	11 32		2 37	3 50	4 28		6 22		8 38		
Lydney Junction ...... arr		9 15	11 39		2 44	3 57	4 35		6 29		8 45		
Lydney .... dep		10 28	1 40				5 8		7 20		8 59		
Gloucester .... arr		11 11	2 18				5 37		7 55		9 25		
Gloucester .... dep		7 50	10 55		1 55		3 30		5 5		7 50		
Lydney .... arr		8 29	11 38		2 27		4 10		5 45		8 12		
Lydney Junction ...... dep		9 19	11 46		2 46		4 40		6 33		9 00		
Lydney Town .... ,,	7 20	9 22	11 40		2 48		4 43		6 36		9 03		9 10
Whitecroft .... ,,	7 27	9 29	11 58				4 51		6 43				9 20
Parkend .... arr	7 29	9 31	11 58				4 58		6 45				
Milkwall (for Clearwell) .. dep	8 0	9 56	12 17				5 14						
Coleford (for Staunton) .. arr	8 5	10 0	12 21				5 18						
Coleford .... dep		8 55							5 55				
Milkwall (for Clearwell) .. ,,		8 59							5 59				
Parkend .... dep	7 50	9 33	12 0						6 46				
Speech House Road ...... ,,	7 44	9 45	12 11						6 53				
Drybrook Road .... ,,	7 53	9 52	12 18		3 1								
Cinderford (New Station) { arr	7 58	9 56	12 22						7 3				
Cinderford (New Station) { dep	8 7	10 1	12 25						7 6				
Drybrook Road .... dep	8 11	10 5	12 30						7 10				
Upper Lydbrook .... ,,	8 19	10 14	12 39						7 19				
Lower Lydbrook .... ,,	M	M	M										
LYDBROOK JUNCTION .. arr	8 26	10 20	12 45						7 25				

Up Trains.		Week Days only.											
		a.m.	a.m.	a.m.	p.m.	p.m.	p.m.	p.m.	p.m.			p.m.	p.m.
LYDBROOK JUNCTION ... dep		8 37		12 6		4 2						7 45	
Lower Lydbrook .... ,,		M		M		M							
Upper Lydbrook .... ,,		8 45		12 14		4 8						7 53	
Drybrook Road .... ,,		8 50		12 31		4 18						8 4	
Cinderford (New Station) { arr		8 59		12 35		4 22						8 8	
Cinderford (New Station) { dep		9 4		12 38		4 25	7 55		5 59			8 11	
Drybrook Road .... dep		9 8		12 42			5 59		6 6			8 15	
Speech House Road ...... ,,		9 15		12 49		4 35	6 6		6 11			8 20	
Parkend .... arr		9 25		12 58		4 44	6 11					8 29	
Milkwall (for Clearwell) .. dep		9 56				5 14							
Coleford (for Staunton) .. arr		10 0				5 18							
Coleford .... dep		8 55		12 33		4 10		5 55					
Milkwall .... ,,		8 59		12 39		4 16		5 59					
Parkend .... dep		9 26		12 59		4 45	6 12	6 17				8 50	9 30
Whitecroft .... ,,	Mxd	9 30		1 1			6 14	6 20				8 53	9 33
Lydney Town .... ,,	7 28	9 37		1 9	2 53	4 53	6 21	6 29				9 1	9 40
Lydney Junction ...... arr		9 40		1 11	2 55	4 57		6 29				9 4	
Lydney .... dep		10 25		1 40		5 8		7 20				8 55	
Gloucester .... arr		11 11		2 18		5 37		7 55				9 25	
Gloucester .... dep		9 42	10 55	12 19	1 55	3 40		5 45				8 55	
Lydney .... arr		8 29	11 38	12 52	2 27	4 10							
Lydney Junction ...... dep		9 42	11 50	1 12	2 50	5 12		6 32					
Severn Bridge (for Blakeney) ,,	7 38	9 49	11 57	1 19	3 3	5 19		6 39					
Sharpness .... ,,	7 45	9 56	12 2	1 25	3 9	5 25		6 55					
Berkeley .... ,,	7 51	10 2		1 31	3 15	5 31		7 1					
BERKELEY ROAD .... arr	7 57	10 8		1 37	3 20	5 37		7 10					

G—Saturdays excepted.

M—Calls when required to set down Passengers on notice being given. Also calls to pick up Passengers, notice being given at the Station.

An early time table of the Severn & Wye and Severn Bridge Railway published in the Gloucester Journal shortly after its inauguration.

Author's Collection

assure you that my task has not been so great as Lord Ducie has represented it to be. I have the benefit of an able vice chairman in my friend Mr. Clegram, I have also faithfully contributed towards the support of the undertaking. We have further had the benefit of good engineers, Messrs. Keeling and Owen and in the consulting engineer Mr. Harrison, and last but not least, we have had exceedingly good contractors in the Hamiltons Windsor Iron Works Company.' Lucy spoke at some length on the subject of the previous bridge schemes and later said 'I mentioned that an Act was obtained by the Great Western

Railway Company, for making a tunnel under the river and my friend Sir Daniel Gooch, who usually succeeds in all the engineering work that he undertakes, is confident of success. We hear a great deal these days of the erratic doings of spirits and I am inclined sometimes to think there may be some truth in mythology. Now should Neptune, who is supposed to hold dominion over the sea, resent the intrusion of the iron horse beneath his domain and his anger takes the form of rending the limestone rock of 'The Shoots', then we shall be very glad to offer the Great Western Railway Company a high and dry way over our bridge for their South Wales traffic to London.'

W.B. Clegram proposed the toast 'The Engineers and Contractors'. He paid tribute to Keeling on whom rested the merit and responsibility and to Messrs. Wells Owen and Reichenbach, the latter having dealt with all the details of the work, supervising the whole structure from the deepest foundation to highest rivet. The contractors were also praised; the erection of the bridge had been a work of great difficulty but the difficulties had been overcome and the greatest possible credit was due to the engineers and contractors.

Keeling responded and said that the problem had occupied his mind for many years since 1859 in regard to a bridge over the river. In 1859 he had been engaged on a survey of the river and the conviction was forced upon him that the only place for a crossing was at the Old Passage or at any point between Wheel Rock or Milkmaid Rock. In 1865 Clegram employed him to survey the river near Sharpness and the result of his observations was, that this was the ideal place for a bridge, but the origin of the idea was entirely due to Clegram. Eventually the work started on the Sharpness side, and he recalled the time of the first accident in the river, he had been away from home and on arriving at Lydney, found a telegram waiting, informing him that one of the piers had been washed away, he was struck with horror but later realised what a benefit the accident had been for it showed that the channel staging should be much stronger. Keeling then paid tribute to Messrs. Sharrock, Earle and Loutitt, praising their skill, cheerfulness and co-operation in all their dealings with each other.

S.H. Loutitt of Hamiltons Windsor Iron Works Company said the directors had shown immense confidence in the engineers and contractors and the Severn Bridge Railway Company's engineers and their assistant, Oscar Reichenbach had afforded his firm the fullest assistance. The contractors relied on Sharrock and Earle and they in turn relied on men who had not failed them. 'Peace has its victories, no less renowned than in war' and for his own part, he would rather have been an engineer of the Severn Bridge than one of the many soldiers they had

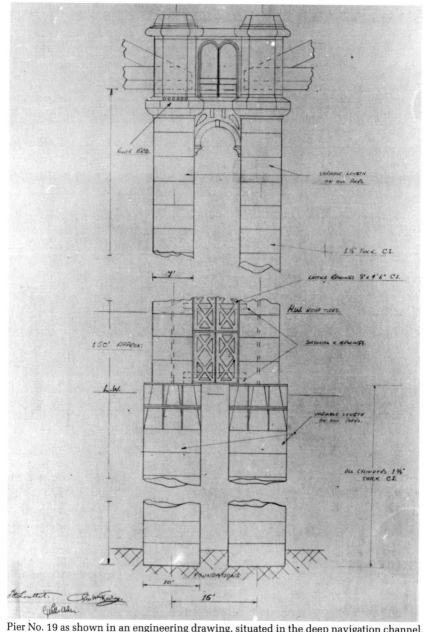

Pier No. 19 as shown in an engineering drawing, situated in the deep navigation channel, height approximately 150 feet from foundation to track level.

District Civil Engineer, British Rail, Gloucester

heard of so much in recent years.

Many of the company called for George Earle, he arose amidst cheers and told the guests that the directors had presented him with a very valuable gold watch, he had simply done his duty, but he appreciated the assistance of the engineers and everyone concerned.

The chairman then proposed 'The Subscribing Companies' to which Charles Thomas, a local director of the Midland Railway Company responded. Lucy then announced he had a further toast to propose, one that was not shown on his list, that of the health of the 'non Subscribing Company' the Great Western Railway Company. He mentioned that the Severn Bridge Railway Company had not been undertaken with any hostility to other interests and that they would welcome any traffic which might be received from Sir Daniel Gooch. Their desire was full co-operation with him and as far as possible to join together to develop the traffic of South Wales. He hoped that when the Severn Tunnel was completed, they would all be invited to its opening.

Sir Daniel Gooch said that the Great Western Railway Company had never shown any antagonism towards the bridge. They were desirous of and agreed to aid in its construction, but cirumstances prevented that aid being given. He hoped the traffic of the company would be fully developed over the bridge with contributions from the Great Western Railway and other interested companies. With regard to the opening of the tunnel, he suggested some of the present company might wish to accompany him in walking through it, but suggested they should bring umbrellas!

W.P. Price proposed the health of the merchants and coal and iron masters of the district and spoke at some length on the trade of the district to which Edward Jones, vice chairman of the Coal Association of South Wales responded. One of the last toasts of the day was proposed by the chairman to the mayors, presidents of chambers of commerce and other visitors. Alderman Jessie Collings, mayor of Birmingham responded. The mayor of Gloucester proposed 'The health of the vice chairman W.B. Clegram' and in his speech paid a glowing tribute to both Lucy and Clegram, who acknowledged the compliment and the proceedings terminated.

The party then proceeded to Sharpness Station and departed for Gloucester by the special train.

During the proceedings the news that the Severn Tunnel headings had been flooded was passed to Sir Daniel Gooch, and unbeknown at the time this disaster was to delay the tunnel project for a considerable period.

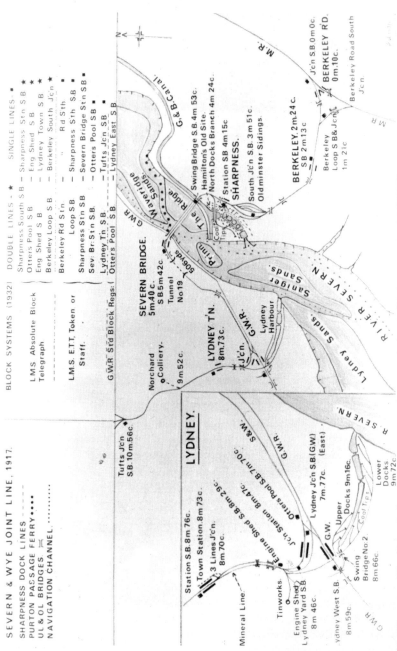

SEVERN & WYE JOINT LINE. 1917.

SHARPNESS DOCK LINES ————
PURTON PASSAGE FERRY ••••
UL & OL BRIDGES ⫴
NAVIGATION CHANNEL ....

BLOCK SYSTEMS (1932)

LMS Absolute Block
LMS Telegraph

LMS. E.T.T, Token or
Staff.

GWR Std Block Regs:

DOUBLE LINES - ■

Sharpness South S B
Otters Pool S B
Eng Shed S B
Berkeley Loop S B
Berkeley Rd Stn —
Loop S B
Sharpness Stn S B
Sev. Br. Stn S B
Lydney Tn S.B.
Otters Pool S B

SINGLE LINES ■

Sharpness Stn S B ——
Eng Shed S B ★
Lydney Town S B ★
Berkeley South Jcn ★
Rd Sth
Sharpness Sth S B ■
Severn Bridge Stn S B ■
Otters Pool S B ■
Tufts Jcn S B ■
Lydney East S B ■

Tufts Jcn
S.B. 10m.56c.

SEVERN BRIDGE.
5m.40 c.
S.B.5m.42c.
Tunnel
No.19

Norchard
Colliery.
9m 52c.

LYDNEY T'N.
8m.73c.
Jc'n.

Lydney
Harbour

LYDNEY.

Station S.B. 8m 76c.
Town Station. 8m.73c.
3 Lines J'c'n.
8m.70c.

Mineral Line.

Tinworks.

Engine Shed /
Lydney Yard S.B
8m 46c.

Lydney West S.B.
8m 59c.

Jc'n Station 8m.47c.
Otters Pool S.B 8m 70c.

Engine Shed S.B.8m 29c.

Lydney Jc'n S.B.(GW.)
7m 77c.

Swing
Bridge No. 2
8m 66c.

(East)

G.W.
Upper
Docks
G.W.
Lower
Docks
9m 72c.

Coal Tips

Docks 9m16c.

S.&W.

G.W.R.

GWR.

GWR.

GWR

R. SEVERN.

Lydney Sands

Saniger Sands

RIVER SEVERN

Lydney Harbour

Primm

Waveridge Sands

Boveds

The Ridge

G. & B. Ca.

Swing Bridge S.B. 4m 53c.
Hamilton's Old Site.
North Docks Branch 4m 24c.
Station SB 4m 15c.

SHARPNESS.

South Jc'n S.B. 3m 51c.
Oldminster Sidings.

BERKELEY. 2m.24 c.
S B 2m13c.

Berkeley
Loop S B & Jc'n
1m 21c.

Jc'n S B 0m 0c.

BERKELEY RD.
0m.10c.

Berkeley Road South
Jcn.

M.R.

M.R

N
W   E
S

The Severn & Wye Joint Railway 1917 giving mileages and details of systems used from Berkeley Road to Lydney Town.
Appendix to Service Time Tables

The end of the Purton Passage ferry

The Purton Passage ferry now closed, had been superseded by the bridge. the ferry had been operated by the Inman family of Lower Etloe, Blakeney, during a period of 200 years. Passengers who had had the occasion to avail themselves of the ferry service of later years and especially during the progress of the bridge would remember that Henry Inman had been captain of the boat and his kindly, unassuming manner, with the respect he had secured in the discharge of his duties, had now earned an appointment under the Severn & Wye and Severn Bridge Railway Company, the announcement of which would be received with satisfaction by his numerous friends.

This appointment was a generous act on the part of the directors of the Company and was a pleasing instance of the general kindly atmosphere, which throughout, had pervaded the undertaking in all its phases.

The Severn Bridge Railway Act discharged the proprietor of the Purton Passage ferry from all liabilities, debts and payments with compensation payable by the Severn & Wye & Severn Bridge Railway Company for loss of business. Henry Inman's appointment with the Company took him high above the channel where his ferry once plied. His was the responsibility for the maintenance of the navigation lights above the main channel and was to remain so for life, in lieu of compensation.

The Severn Bridge Railway Act contained a clause in respect of the navigation lights, that they should be displayed in the manner pre-scribed by the Elder Brethren of Trinity House.

Traces of the Purton Passage ferry can still be seen at Purton Quay where a ramp leads down from the quay to a small cobbled road across the mud flats to a deep water anchorage. The ferry was in turn served by a small station or halt known as Gatcombe on the South Wales line, quite near to the quay. Old milestones near Viney Hill and Yorkley denotes the distance to Purton Passage and these leading from the ferry gives the mileage to Coleford.

Further celebrations

On Wednesday 22 October George Earle who had resided in Blakeney throughout the duration of the project was invited to a dinner at the Bird in Hand Inn, Blakeney in which the Reverend A.D. Pringle had taken the initiative in organising a public subscription. T. Teesdale of Kingsland (a shareholder of the Severn & Wye & Severn Bridge Railway Company) presided and the vice chairman was S. Charley. Amongst the

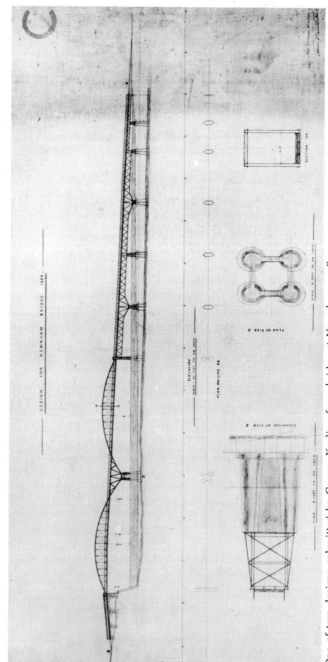

One of two designs submitted by George Keeling for a bridge at Newnham-on-Severn.

Severn Bridge (for Blakeney) Station 1905; the tall signal box was later demolished and a standard type box installed near the right-hand end of the platform.

Author's Collection

guests were Keeling and Reichenbach. Charley, in proposing a toast to Earle, remarked that he hoped that Earle would, in the near future, be employed on another Severn Bridge, preferably a road bridge at Newnham.

During the same week sixty redundant workers who had been employed on the bridge, were entertained to a supper at the Kings Head Inn, Blakeney, the expense being borne by Keeling. His arrival at the proceedings was heralded by lusty cheers but the question of their future employment was doubtful.

References to Chapter Four

1. *Gloucester Journal* Saturday 18 October 1879.
2. *Gloucester Journal* Saturday 25 October 1879.

CHAPTER FIVE

The White Elephant

Starvation and violence in the Forest

The Forest of Dean over the past nine years had been plunged into a turmoil of industrial unrest and the miners' strikes had created distress unprecedented in the Forest's long history of mining. The strikers during this period, led by their agent, Timothy Mountjoy, had refused to accept wage cuts and instead, demanded fifteen per cent rises, which ended in strikes and lock-outs.

In March 1874, the miners refused to submit to further wage cuts and preferred to work part time, while merchants were complaining at the high cost of Forest coal. At a mass meeting of miners at the Archery Ground near the Speech House, resolutions were passed, requesting the employers to withdraw their proposed twenty-five per cent cuts and eventually the miners settled for reductions of ten per cent.

By the middle of 1874, the depression had assumed country-wide proportions, and only a few miners in the Forest were working two days per week, and at a miners' meeting in August, attended by 3–4,000 miners, there was bitter opposition by union men against the non-union men, the union men claiming that non-union men were idlers and when they did work, they clamoured for more money than those who had paid their dues!

The Severn Bridge project and the work on the approaches, had contributed to relieving the distress in the district, 300 men had been employed on the approaches alone and in 1879, there was some conceern that work was now rapidly approaching completion.

Timothy Mountjoy of Bilson Green, who had been elected by the miners in 1872 as their agent, learned early in the year that his services were to be discontinued, a decision taken by the miners' union executive, who reported that there appeared to be a collapse of the Forest union. The distress in the Forest in 1879 was now most acute; during the past two years, there had been a mass exodus of miners from the area to seek their fortunes in the North, but many returned to face starvation.

During this period, many acts of violence were perpetrated, one miner living at Bradley Hill, near Blakeney, who possessed a few sheep to assist in the struggle to survive, awoke one morning to find all his sheep had been brutally slaughtered and their legs broken, while the landlord of the Kings Head Inn, Blakeney, discovered two of his cows' tails had been cut off short in the night and had bled to death.

A scheme was introduced under the Poor Law to employ the out of work miners on the construction of roads in the Forest area for the pittance of 1s. 6d. per day, indeed a pittance when their earnings as miners was 10s. per day. Many refused to work under these terms and those who did, were abused by their own friends, one miner who accepted these terms was brutally kicked insensible at Bream and Inspector Chipp of Lydney was sent to investigate this vicious act.

Stonebreakers were employed at Milkwall and Howbeach Quarries to provide stone for the roads, the normal rate for the quarry employees being 1s. 6d. per cubic yard, but under the Poor Law scheme, the miners received 9d. per cubic yard, in the case of a man supporting a wife, an additional 2d. was paid for each child up to the age of fourteen years. The day often started with an issue of bread and cheese to the miners, as many arrived at the site without breakfast or food for the day.

Much of the money needed to pay miners engaged on this project came from donations from charitable institutions, the churches, and other sources, and when funds ran low, work was suspended until sufficient funds had been accumulated to enable work to proceed.

In May 1879, 216 sacks of potatoes were distributed at Parkend to the hungry and as many as 500 women arrived at the distribution centre with every receptacle they could find to receive their allocation.

During the week of 15 June, a Whitsuntide gift of one pound of tea and one pound of sugar was distributed to every poor woman in the townships of West Dean, aged seventy and upwards. Tea was donated by William Simpson of Liverpool and sugar by the grocers of Coleford, Gloucester, Cheltenham and Evesham. The Reverends W.H. Taylor and S.G. Edwards undertook the distribution in their respective areas, two hundredweight of peas, beans and other seeds for planting was also distributed, donated by F.A. Dickson & Son of Chester.

In spite of the events of the last few years, the directors of the Severn & Wye and Severn Bridge Railway Company were now looking forward confidently to the dawning of a new era of prosperity for the Company as well as the Forest of Dean. Early reports in 1879 indicated that shipments of grain were now being transported over the Severn Bridge to South Wales at a considerable economy in transport costs to the corn merchants of Sharpness. Regarding passenger traffic, it was noted that people residing in the Coleford area wishing to travel to Bristol, found that fares were rather on the high side, and many preferred to travel by

69

the Great Western route and the New Passage Ferry.

Safety of the bridge in doubt

Following the Tay Bridge disaster, G.W. Keeling had written to *The Times* in an endeavour to reassure the public as to the safety of the Severn Bridge, to which Lord Powerscourt had replied, but in the process, had misinterpreted Keeling's presentation of the facts.

To set troubled minds at rest, S. Sharrock of Hamiltons, Windsor Iron Works Limited, wrote the following letter to *The Times*[1]

Sir,

In *The Times* of this morning, I noticed a letter from Lord Powerscourt, which may cause additional and groundless anxiety to the public minds as to the safety of the Severn Bridge.

I write to say his Lordship was undoubtedly misinformed or was not himself understood in the question he asked, as to the cylinders of the above bridge, the exact truth being the very opposite of his Lordship's statement. As a matter of fact, the cylindrical piers of the Severn Bridge are virtually one solid structure from bottom to top; the largest pillars are 10′ in diameter, formed of short lengths 4′ long by 10′ diameter, and these short lengths are not merely superimposed on top of one another. After having been brought to a true face in the lathe, they are bolted together by 56 bolts $1\frac{1}{8}''$ diameter at each joint, thus ensuring a great and reliable lateral strength, as if the cylinders were one solid pillar from bottom to top; in fact, these pillars, when bolted together and before filled with concrete, would have such strength and continuity of structure that they would, if laid horizontally and merely supported at their extreme ends, carry themselves like a tubular girder.

His Lordship did wisely, however, I think, in raising the question of lateral strength in these structures, as it is quite in vain to merely provide strength against the vertical loading of our bridges without taking into account and scientifically providing for the maximum lateral forces due to violent winds and other causes.

In every part of the Severn Bridge from the highest point of the superstructure to the solid rock foundation, the lateral strength necessary to resist the terrible winds of the Severn Estuary, has been provided for, as well as for the maximum vertical loading; and being familiar with all its details, as well as having considered its powers of resisting all the destructive forces that are in the remotest degree likely to come against it from any quarter, I doubt not, that the gales, furious as they are, will pass over it harmlessly.

I am Sir,

Yours faithfully,

Samuel Sharrock, M.I.C.E.
Manager of Works and Engineer
to the contractors who built
the Severn Bridge,
Hamiltons Windsor Iron Works Ltd.
8 Old Jewrey,
London, E.C.

1 January 1880.

Keeling, in reply to Lord Powerscourt's letter endorsed Sharrock's statement.

The first half-yearly meeting of the Severn & Wye and Severn Bridge Railway Company

At the meeting at the Canal Office, Gloucester, on Wednesday 25 February 1880[2] Lucy moved the adoption of the accounts, stating that the accounts extended as far as the amalgamation was concerned from 17 October to 31 December and therefore gave but a very inadequate notion of what would be, as he hoped, the future of the Company.

The Company had not been able to fully unilise Sharpness Docks for that trade which they had always looked forward to as being very important to the undertaking, owing to the coal tip at Sharpness not having been completed until quite recently. Shareholders should not be disappointed if they did not find a large accession of trade during the next six to twelve months; indeed he though it might take up to two years to develop anything like a large trade.

Very much depended on circumstances beyond the control of the directors. A notable instance was the trade of the Forest of Dean. During the past month the traffic over the bridge had fallen off very much, owing to an advance in the price of coal and a day or two ago, he was sorry to see a strike was being contemplated and due to take place at one of the colleries.

He thought there may be some shareholders who were anxious for the safety of the bridge, remembering the recent Tay disaster, but it was a great source of satisfaction to the directors that the bridge had been examined by a competent and independent gentleman who

71

pronounced it safe, and after recent gales, the bridge had been examined by the Company's engineer, the result of which was highly satisfactory.

Keeling reported that the structure of the bridge was in sound condition and that further work was being continued in extending the cast iron cross bracings on the piers to a greater height, timber dolphins were also being erected round the piers in the navigation channel.

Keeling honoured

Shortly after the opening of the Severn Bridge, a proposal was made to entertain G.W. Keeling with a banquet at Lydney, but owing to the death of one of the directors, Henry Crawshay of Oaklands Park, Newnham-on-Severn, the matter was postponed.

Owing to the important nature of the bridge project, it was thought that the matter should not be passed over without some compliment to the engineer and a testimonial was subscribed to by the residents of Lydney and district. On Saturday 1 May, the formal presentation was made at the National School Room, Lydney.

The testimonial consisted of an elegant silver centre piece for candelabrum with glasses for flowers. Its base consisted of a plateau, on one side was engraved the outline of the Severn Bridge and the opposite side bore the following inscription:

'Presented to George William Keeling, Esq., Civil Engineer, by his friends and neighbours, to record their hearty congratulations on his successful completion of the Severn Bridge, opened on 17 October 1879.'

The testimonial was supplied by Messrs. Martin & Son of Cheltenham at a cost of 100 guineas.

J.A. Grahame Clarke said that he had long been connected with the Severn & Wye Company, almost from the Dark Ages, when it was a miserable little tramway, and he had had ample opportunity to witness the work of George Keeling, not only connected with the bridge but with the whole of the system. He had seen the outcome of his genious, first in the splendid viaduct at Lydbrook and secondly the Severn Bridge. He considered the Severn Bridge to be one of the greatest triumphs in engineering skill in the kingdom, and unlike the Tay Bridge, it had stood the test and was sound and secure. At this point the presentation was made.

Keeling, who was heartily cheered, acknowledged the kindness of his friends and remarked that prior to coming forward for the presentation, he felt he had much to say, but was now fully conscious of an extreme state of nervousness. He thanked the speaker for his kind remarks and those responsible for the presentation. He spoke of his many exploits on previous surveys in the river and the fact that he was always glad to set foot on dry land after being out in the river. He remarked that all men connected with the river, pilots and masters etc., entertained great prejudice against the bridge and as each pier was being erected, would shout on passing 'When you come to the next one, you'll find out your mistake': but nevertheless the bridge was completed.

Keeling also outlined the dangers of the river with its great eddies · and vortexes near Wheel Rock, sufficient to seize and capsize a boat, and recalled the legend of the area, of the fiddlers from the Forest, who had crossed to the east bank and on their return, their boat was capsized near Wheel Rock, all were drowned, but on occasions, they could still be heard fiddling.

Further speeches were made by Sir James Campbell, W.J. Brain of Trafalgar Colliery and George Baker Keeling.[3]

The storm clouds gather

Lucy reported in February 1881 at the third half-yearly meeting, that all facilities were now avaliable at Sharpness Docks, the Dock Company had made a reduction in dock dues and the directors were now looking forward to large shipments of Welsh coal to Sharpness.

But at the fourth half-yearly meeting in August, the first rumble of distant thunder was heard when a number of Severn & Wye Section shareholders told the directors they they were disillusioned with the amalgamation of the two companies. Lucy's report explained that the Company's expenditure was up for the first half of 1881, owing to the severe winter, but he ended with a confident note that Welsh coal shipments to Sharpness were continuing to improve slowly. With regard to the passenger traffic, the Company had promoted a guide book to encourage tourists to the Forest, and 5,000 copies had been sold and 2,000 more ordered.

The disillusioned shareholders

The fifth half-yearly meeting[4] was held at the Canal Office, Gloucester on Friday 24 February 1882. At this meeting Lucy explained two Bills to be promoted in Parliament, the South Wales and Severn Bridge Railway Bill and the Thames and Severn Railway Bill.

The first commenced by a junction with the Severn & Wye and Severn Bridge Railway, one and a half miles from Lydney via Mon-

73

mouth and Abergavenny to Talybont, joining with the Brecon line at Abergavenny, designed as a through arterial line with a view to giving a second communication between South Wales and London and the south west coast of England. He believed the promoters had succeeded in placing the line in the best practicable position.

By means of this line, the Company felt that unless they could get access, and better access that then existed, to South Wales and the south west of England, their property was not likely to increase or improve in value.

The Thames and Severn Railway was designed to supply a link by commencing at Stroud and passing along on the site of the existing Thames and Severn Canal to Siddington, joining the Swindon and Marlborough line. Should this line be made, it would give a very direct run down to Andover and on to Southampton and Portsmouth. It would also give a second route via the South Western line from Andover to London, but not as direct as one might desire.

Another and better route was afforded by passing the east Gloucester line and joining the London and North Western Railway at Yarnton Junction to Bletchley and from Bletchley to London. Speaking as one of the promoters of the Severn Wye & Severn Bridge Railway Bill he mentioned that some of the directors had accompanied him on a visit to South Wales earlier in the week, and there they had found a considerable number of people in sympathy with the enterprise, whose great desire was to see a second line competing for traffic between London and South Wales.

On concluding the directors report, he remarked that the directors had resolved on a dividend of half a per cent for the whole year, the dividend being paid on 20 March. B.S. Stock as one of the shareholders of the Severn & Wye Section felt that the Company's affairs were in a very bad state, in fact, he could only see one comforting assurance in the accounts, and that was that the debentures and debenture stock were completely safe.

The united account of the Company showed a profit of £820 after payment of interest, but referring to his own section, nothing appeared to him to be much worse. The result of the arrangements between the two sections during the half year, seventy per cent to the Severn & Wye and thirty per cent to the Severn Bridge had been a profit of £875 to the Bridge Section and a loss of fifty pounds to the Severn & Wye. If one could see that this would be the termination of this present state of affairs, one would not say a word, but he would ask those who understood figures, what would be their condition now if instead of seventy per cent during the greater part of the half year for the Severn &

74

Wye and thirty per cent to the Severn Bridge, they had taken fifty-five per cent and forty-five per cent? According to his showing, the profit to the bridge would be £875 and the loss to the Severn & Wye would be £600.

Lucy remarked that he thought Stock's figures were a little out, but Stock remained adamant on his theory, he thought the Severn & Wye debt would go on increasing year by year, reaching an irretrievable position. He could not conceive how any gentlemen who met together in conference on the terms of amalgamation could have agreed to those terms, because they must have seen, or ought to have seen by some calculation or other, what they were doing, before consenting to the state of affairs that existed. If they examined why this was done, they would find the capital accounts did not warrant it, the mileage did not warrant it, nor with the position of the Great Western Railway, did the prospects of the bridge warrant it. He would sooner have had no connection with the bridge, unless a probationary period was allowed to examine what was being done and what advantage would be derived. It appeared to him that they had something staring them in the face and were powerless to do anything about it. The dividend ordered that day he thought was wrong, the Company should keep all the money it could and it appeared that the only way to avoid trouble, was to sell their line.

With regard to the new line, he said they thought they were rushing into a very good thing in running over the Severn Bridge, but if they had only known of the sectional differences which would arise, it would tell lies. He thought there must be some uncommonly clever men in the Severn Bridge Section to have cajoled the Severn & Wye directors into accepting such terms as they now had without any trial period or any time to judge how things might turn out.

They had a 'white elephant' in the Severn Bridge and if it did not tread the Severn & Wye people into dust and ashes, he would be very much mistaken. Lucy remarked that he had announced the dividend for the information of the shareholders. His opinion on the amalgamation was that it had been carried out in a fair and equitable manner. He thought the Severn & Wye accounts showed worse perhaps than they really were and required a little explanation. There was a very small proportion of loan capital on the Severn Bridge fortunately for the proprietors, but in the case of the Severn & Wye they had £175,000 worth of debentures and certain fixed engagements which had to be discharged every year. Therefore it would follow, the receipts being equal, there was a state of indebtedness from one Company to another. He wished the Severn & Wye capital stood in a different position and pointed out the benefits of the bridge. He thought they should do their utmost to develop traffic and reduce expenses as much as possible, nurse their undertaking and show they possessed a property which must, some time or other be of benefit as an important highway between London and South Wales.

The storm breaks

The sixth half-yearly meeting[5] was held at the Royal Hotel, College Green, Bristol on Friday 25 August 1882, a venue formerly favoured by the Severn & Wye Railway and Canal Company. The Canal Office at Gloucester had first been used by the Severn Bridge Railway Company in 1872, until the fifth meeting of the Severn & Wye and Severn Bridge Railway Company.

The meeting commenced with a gloomy note and the promise of worse to come. Lucy presiding, expressed his great disappointment at the untoward withdrawl of both the South Wales and Severn Bridge Railway and Thames and Severn Railway Bills. He said at the last meeting the directors and shareholders were congratulating themselves that two desirable railway links would soon be established. With regard to the future, he hoped other persons might come forward and renew schemes of a similar character. The only new feature he could speak of in the Forest was the establishment of a new works at Whitecroft by the Pyramid Electric Company, for the preparation of electrical apparatus and telegraph works. He believed them to be undertaken by persons of responsible position and their business might lead to increased trade. He did not like to speculate upon the future, he was so disappointed at the lines of railway not being sanctioned, that he could only say he hoped for the best.

When Lucy announced that the trade of the last year showed a deficit of £1,463 a shareholder, W.F. Brookman, expressed his disappointment that things were deteriorating from bad to worse. He looked upon the Company as without prospect for the future unless trade came to it in the way suggested by the chairman. He did not see any just reason why the line should remain open just for the benefit of a few Forest traders, he would rather see the concern closed down.

When he first joined the Company, there were nine directors, six of whom came from Bristol, and at that time the Company were paying three per cent; at the moment there were only two Bristol men on the Board, not a fair representation of Bristol's interests.

The chairman spoke for some length in an attempt to boost the morale of the shareholders, but referring again to the Forest of Dean, he

PURTON & SHARPNESS,

GLOUCESTERSHIRE.

CATALOGUE

OF THE

VALUABLE PLANT,

COMPLETE, AS USED IN THE CONSTRUCTION OF THE

SEVERN BRIDGE.

Locomotive and Portable Engines; 2 Costly and Superior Air Bells, with their Boilers, Blowing Engines, and other appliances complete, as used for sinking the cylinders of piers under air compression; Steam and other Cranes; Goliath and other Gantries; Punching and Shearing Machine; Single, Double, and Treble purchase Crab Winches; Screw and Hydraulic Jacks; Lime Mill by *Clayton and Shuttleworth*; Screw and Hydraulic *White's* patent endless Chain; Steam Pile Drivers and Engines; Barges; Iron and Copper fastened Boats; Anchors and Chains; several tons of Nuts and Bolts; Scrap Iron and Rails; Contractors' Waggons; Corrugated Sheet Iron and Wooden Buildings; *Siebe and Gorman's* Diving Apparatus and Dresses; Divers' Tools; Centrifugal and other Pumps; a large number of Spruce Deals; about 60,000 cubic feet of Pitch Pine in baulk, of superior growth, very best selected, in excellent condition, and easy of transit by rail or water; Smiths' and Fitters' Tools; which will be

SOLD BY AUCTION

BY

Messrs. Stephenson, Alexander, & Co.

Commencing on TUESDAY, the 29th JUNE, at 11.30 a.m., and continuing daily at the same hour until the whole is sold.

Order of Sale.

TUESDAY, 29th.—Timber, Materials, and Plant at Purton Passage.
WEDNESDAY, 30th.—Machinery and Plant at Sharpness.
THURSDAY, July 1st.—Timber and remaining Plant at Sharpness.

Catalogues may be had upon application at the principal Hotels at Lydney, Sharpness, Berkeley, Gloucester, and Bristol; Messrs. PITMAN & EDWARDS, 5, Newman's Court, Cornhill, London; Mr. GEORGE EARLE, Manager of the Hamilton Windsor Iron Co., Limited, Sharpness (who will shew the Lots); or upon application to the Auctioneer at Cardiff.

15

Lot.			
267	Snatch Block, 10in. ...	...	...
8	About 3¼ cwt. Chain, ½in. ...		...
9	Ditto 10 Fathoms Wire Rope		...
270	Ladder, 44ft. ...	...	...
1	Quantity Wrought Iron Shoes and sundries ...		...
2	About 2 ton Wrought Scrap Iron		...
3	About Three tons Channel Iron Angles and Blocks ...		...
4	Sundries ...	...	...
5	Ditto ...	...	...
6	Ditto ...	...	...
7	Ditto ...	...	...
8	Ditto ...	...	...
9	Ditto ...	...	...
280	Ditto ...	...	...
1	Very excellent Lime Mill by *Clayton and Shuttleworth*, now lying at Lidney Harbour.		
2	Wooden Shed covering same.		
3			
4			
5			
6			
7			
8			

The Timber included in this day's sale is all on the Purton Passage side of the Severn, and can be either shipped, rafted, or conveyed by rail.

End of First Day's Sale.

18

Lot	
291	Gantry Traveller, incomplete
2	Cast Iron Cylinder, 10 ft. dia., 4 ft. deep x 1½ in.
3	Ditto, 7 ft. dia., 4 ft. deep x 1¼ in.
4	Ditto, 7 ft. dia., 4 ft. deep x 1¼ in.
5	Ditto, 6 ft. dia., 4 ft. deep x 1 in.
6	Ditto, 6 ft. dia., 4ft. deep x 1 in.
7	Costly and superior Air Bell, 5 ft. dia., suitable for sinking Cylinders in the construction of the largest iron bridges in the world, with Blowing Engine and Boiler and Apparatus complete
8	Ditto
301	Cast Iron Diagonal Bracing, 15 ft. x 13 ft. 9 in. x 1½ in.
2	Pair Wrought Iron Waggon Wheels
3	Ditto
4	Ten tons of Cylinder Weights, 4 cwt. each
5	Ten tons ditto
6	Ten tons ditto
7	Ten tons ditto
8	Ten tons ditto
310	Ten tons ditto
1	Ten tons ditto
2	Fifteen tons ditto
3	Cast Iron Drilling Post, 13 ft. 6 in.
4	Steam Travelling Crane, to lift 2 tons, with spring balance, steam and water gauge, &c., by Appleby

---

17

SECOND DAY'S SALE.

Commencing at the Yard near the Gasometer, adjoining the Gloucester and Berkeley Canal, Sharpness Docks. Intending Purchasers should book to Sharpness Dock Station.

Lot	
289	An excellent Locomotive Saddle Tank Steam Engine, 8 in. cylinders, 10 in. stroke, boiler of best Lowmoor iron plates, four wheels (coupled) 2 ft. 5½ in. diameter, copper fire box and brass tubes, by Fletcher, Jennings & Co., Whitehaven, recently been thoroughly repaired and placed in good working order
290	Very superior and powerful Locomotive Saddle Tank Steam Engine, "Forrester," 10 in. cylinders, 20 in. stroke, fitted with Ramsbottom's steel piston rings, boiler of best Lowmoor iron plates, six wheels (coupled) 3 ft. dia., copper fire box and brass tubes, by Fletcher, Jennings & Co., of Whitehaven, very recently overhauled, and in good working condition

Four pages from the catalogue of the sale of plant gives a brief idea of some of the equipment used in the construction work. Henry Inman's ferry boat also came under the hammer at the same sale.

Author's Collection

The elevated railway branch from the North Docks to the coal tip in the main dock during construction in the 1880's and demolished nearly a century later.

Cyril Savage

thought there was not sufficient materials in the Forest to supply enough trade to make the Company remunerative. They must look to extraneous sources, which they could only get at over the bridge.

A number of shareholders queried the salaries of £600 and £400 per annum paid to the general manager and secretary respectively, even George Baker Keeling's pension of £533 came under their fire, but Lucy said he thought the affairs of the Company were economically managed and the directors did not receive one farthing. F. Roper, a shareholder, remarked that when he first took up shares in the Company, his annual dividend was seventy pounds, from year to year it had dwindled and in spite of all representations made by himself and a few others, fresh schemes were forced on and at the general meetings they had abundant promises supported by facts and statistics as to the future traffic and the general improvement of the Company's business, and in fact they were given to understand that they were suffering from the want of extension. He need not tell the shareholders how utterly and thoroughly baseless all these arguments had proved, even though they were put forward as facts and supported by statistics.

The chairman interposed saying that he gathered from Roper's remarks that he impugned the conduct of the former directors of the Severn & Wye Company. Roper suggested that there should be an

78

Lydney Town Station staff pose on the platform, date unknown, but long before Beeching came.

Author's Collection

A strange sight at Lydney, a Johnson 0-6-0 locomotive of the Midland Railway hired by the Severn and Wye Company to deal with an upsurge in mineral traffic prior to the Company going into liquidation in 1894.

Author's Collection

2039, ready to proceed to Sharpness, waits near Lydney Town Station.

infusion of new blood into the Company and moved 'That taking as an index of the incompetency of the directors of the Severn & Wye Section, the fact that no dividend has been paid for more than eight and a half years to the original shareholders, a meeting be called for the purpose of appointing new directors for the Severn & Wye Section or to adopt such measures as may be desired fit.' Lucy thought it impossible to put the resolution before the meeting, the directors had been elected for a specified period and at the next meeting there would be an election of officers, the Severn & Wye directors then retiring, and only then would the time be for Mr. Roper to take action.

Roper remarked there was a rider added to his motion 'or to adopt such measures as may be deemed fit'. He thought there should be a special general meeting to give shareholders the opportunity for asking questions and raising subjects of discussion in reference to the lamentable state to which they had been brought. The chairman repeated that the motion could not be submitted and at this point Roper left the meeting in a rage.

Stewart Fripp said he was sorry to see Roper leave the proceedings. He (Roper) had always told him he was totally opposed to the

Sharpness Swing Bridge open to admit canal traffic as shown in an old postcard of 1904.

Author's Collection

Lydney Town Station signal box and level crossing; the gentleman with the wheelbarrow really did follow the horse and cart!

Author's Collection

amalgamation of 1879. In May of that year, notices and forms of proxy were sent out to every individual shareholder in the Severn & Wye; not one single proxy was sent in against the scheme. A meeting was held which Roper did not attend and neither did he send in a proxy. He never uttered a word against the amalgamation, but when things turned out adversely, he could be wise after the event. He went there that day and spoke of the directors of the Severn & Wye Section as if they were only interested in taking their guineas, Roper had no right, and he was sorry he was not there to hear it — to bring charges against a body of men who, having invested their thousands, had done their best and devoted their time and energies to revive the prosperity of the concern. He stated Roper could have disposed of his shares, many years ago at a good price and this he declined to do.

The meeting closed with a vote of thanks from the chairman.

More failures

On 21 December 1882, a deputation representing the promoters of the West of England and South Wales Railway met in Cardiff when Lucy and Riddiford, Solicitor for the promoters, waited upon the Parliamentary Committee of the Cardiff Town Council to enlist their support to the Bill in its passage through Parliament, G.A. Stone, the mayor of Cardiff presided. Riddiford explained the route of the proposed line; commencing at Swindon, where it joins the London and South Western Railway, from Swindon by means of running powers over the Swindon and Cheltenham Railway, it passes to Siddington near Cirencester. From this point, a new line is to be constructed to Nailsworth and then by running powers over the Midland Railway and Severn Bridge Railway to Lydney. From Lydney, a new line is to be constructed via Tintern, Usk and Newport to Bassalleg. Running powers are sought from Bassalleg which will give the Company access to Cardiff and the Taff Vale system.

A further scheme, in no way connected with the West of England, is for constructing a railway up the Rhymney Valley from Cardiff to Machen and Risca. This line would join eventually, the West of England system.[6]

On 9 January 1883, Messrs. Wilton and Riddiford, solicitors for the promoters of the West of England and South Wales scheme, announced the postponement of the Bill to another session. They informed the interested parties that their decision was influenced by the absence of that amount of encouragement which the promoters naturally expected from South Wales. They thanked the mayors of Cardiff, Newport and

Lydney Docks in its heyday, little remains to suggest that this was once a thriving port.
Author's Collection

The bridge looking very resplendent following a new coat of paint in the 1950's. The last bolt tightened by W.C. Lucy in 1879 was for many years painted red.

R. Huxley

Swansea for the facilities they accorded them in making known the project.

Once again, another attempt by the Severn & Wye and Severn Bridge Railway Company to break out from the Forest had failed and once again, for reasons beyond their control.

A short lived revival

At the seventh half-yearly meeting[7] on 23 February 1883, Lucy reported that the last half-year's accounts were the best since amalgamation, with an increase in revenue amounting to £1,237, the improvement being mainly due to minerals and merchandise, though passenger receipts showed a slight excess. The shipment of Welsh coal was still smaller than expected, but had also shown a slight increase.

The chairman moved the adoption of the report and said he was sorry to have to refer to the abandonment of the lines of railway projected into South Wales. Owing to pressure of time and numerous other circumstances,the Bill had been abandoned, it might be re-introduced next session, even though it had failed twice previously, nevertheless, the directors would do everything within their power to make the bridge part of a through line of communication, between London and South Wales. Since the completion of the bridge, the Company was in a much more independent position and had succeeded in penetrating the frontiers of the Great Western Railway which surrounded them.

It was impossible to say to what extent the traffic on the Severn & Wye had been increased by the bridge, but so far as the accounts went, they showed that the increase was about eighteen per cent and there was every reason to believe it should continue to do so.

H.W. Hartnell, a shareholder, asked the directors whether they had approached the Great Western Railway with figures to prove it would be to that Company's advantage to bring coal to Bristol via the bridge in preference to the Gloucester route. The Severn Tunnel would not be completed for two-and-a-half years or more, and during the interim period, the Severn & Wye and Severn Bridge Railway should endeavour to get as much of the trade in coal to Bristol as soon as possible, and if necessary, they should reduce charges in order to do this.

Lucy said that the directors would make a note of the suggestion, but he might mention that the Great Western Railway Company had not given any facilities for the transmission of produce of any kind over the bridge; when approached, the Great Western Railway had always answered 'We have running powers over the Midland Railway.' He would also mention with reference to the attitude of the Great Western

4300 Class locomotive, No. 7307, leaves the bridge with a Bristol–Cardiff passenger train during Sunday working. Note the fine work of the stone mason in the ornamental finials matching the cast iron finials on the bridge.

R. Huxley

Locomotive 6308 leaves Severn Bridge Station with the Cardiff–Bristol train, the occasion being when the Severn Tunnel was closed for Sunday maintenance work.

R. Huxley

14XX Class locomotive No. 1426 takes the Berkeley Road to Lydney Town train into Severn Bridge Station on a summer afternoon in the 1950's.

D. Knight

Railway towards them, that when the pier at Portskewett was destroyed by fire, they supplied a service of trains for the Great Western Railway for a fortnight or three weeks. This service gave great satisfaction, but when they suggested that they should be permitted to run two trains permanently, the Great Western Railway Company declined.

The report was adopted and the meeting terminated.

The Company in Chancery

Hardly had Lucy announced this revival in the fortunes of his Company, when another wave of miners strikes hit the Forest and Lucy's next report[8] came as a bombshell to the shareholders at a general meeting in Bristol. He said the directors in their last half-year's report were able to refer to the recovery of traffic and the Company's ability to pay all interest upon loans and debenture stock to the end of December, and it was therefore with great regret that they now found it necessary to state that owing to the long continued strikes of the colliers in the Forest, the receipts of the first quarter suffered to a considerable extent. In consequence of this serious loss of revenue, the directors were unable to renew or replace the debentures falling due in the half year.

In one instance, viz., that of E. Viner Ellis of Gloucester, a judgment was obtained and a petition to the High Court of Justice had since been filed by him, under which the Board had been appointed managers and the general manager and secretary, joint receivers.

The management of the line would continue practically as before, except that all receipts would be accounted for to the court who would order a distribution of surplus from time to time.

The directors very much regretted the circumstances which had brought this about but they felt that admitting as they were forced to, the necessity of the steps taken, the matter had been brought under the notice of the court in the way least injurious to the general interest of both debenture and shareholders.

A reduction of 6d. per ton had been made in the coal rates from South Wales to Sharpness Docks, which it was believed would have a beneficial effect on that source of traffic.

The maintenance of the docks, canal and permanent way had been drastically reduced, but it was necessary to take advantage of the fine weather and paint a considerable portion of the Severn Bridge. Only a small portion of re-laying had been carried out and sixty-five per cent of the main line and branches were laid with steel rails.

The sixth half-yearly meeting

Thirty-four shareholders attended the sixth half-yearly meeting held at the Royal Hotel on Friday 26 August 1883. Lucy remarked that the Welsh coal traffic had not shown the augmentation he had hoped. The returns for the past half-year had been 6,862 tons against 7,478 tons the previous year, but arrangements had lately been made with the Great Western whereby a reduction would be made in the rates and that reduction would, he hoped, result in an increase in their export trade.

He thought it right not to conceal from them the fact that the present position of their coal tip at Sharpness was not in a most desirable position. Vessels at the dock had increased considerably in size and he might mention that, during the first eleven weeks prior to the eighteenth of that month, out of 80,000 tons that left Sharpness, 40,000 tons were loaded in ships too deep to load at the present tip. Should this continue, the Company should approach the Canal Company in the hope that a new tip might be erected in a deeper part of the docks.

The chairman referred to the recent strikes in the Forest and depression in the tin plate trade and said this had diminished the receipts at a time when a heavy amount of debentures were falling due — the amount of debentures during the year having been £73,000. Of this £5,700 formed part of the bridge debentures, in renewing which there was no difficulty inasmuch as they were guaranteed. This, with the shortness of capital to run the concern, had caused great anxiety to the directors, and after taking the advice of several persons interested in the undertaking, and also consulting some experts in London, they had, with great reluctance, arrived at the conclusion that the only safe and proper mode of procedure was to get the protection of the Court of Chancery.

As they were aware, the Company was now in Chancery and their object must be to conduct the management, which still remained in the hands of the directors, although controlled by the Court of Chancery, in the cheapest and most economical manner possible, which could only be accomplished by an infusion of more capital.

S.J. Sayce, a shareholder, proposed that a committee should be appointed to confer with the directors upon the present position of the Company, owing to its unsatisfactory condition. Messrs. S.J. Sayce, T. Brookman, H. Bennett, W. Hathaway and J.T. Exley were nominated; the proposal was seconded by H. Bennett and carried unanimously.

B.S. Stock complained that the profits of the two sections were not clearly set forth in the accounts and thought the directors were positively making a section of the bond-holders and shareholders their enemies. He asked the chairman to state fairly the receipts of each section, to which the chairman referred him to his previous explanations, and after a brief consultation with the directors, said they were perfectly willing to acquiesce in the suggestions made.

The report was adopted and the chairman terminated the meeting in the usual manner.

1884   The ninth half-yearly meeting

Fifty-four shareholders attended the ninth meeting[9] of shareholders at Bristol on 22 February.

Lucy moved the adoption of the directors report previously published. He expressed his regrets at the passing of Sir Samuel Marling, Bart., a director of the Bridge Section, who had been connected with the Company since 1872, and informed the shareholders that the vacancy on the Board had been filled by Sir Samuel's son, Sir William Henry Marling, Bart.

Referring to the accounts, Lucy said that the expenditure during the last half year, had been £13,438 2s. 9d. against £13,052 for the corresponding previous half year. The increase had risen in consequence considerable amount of dredging required at Lydney Basin, and also with re-laying the old iron permanent way with steel rails.

The capital account showed a total expenditure of £385. 13s. 6d., but out of that, there was a credit of £250 received from the sale of Oldminster Arms (near Sharpness) which of course had nothing to do with the Severn & Wye Section, but which belonged to the deed of amalgamation, to the joint capital account.

After allowing for the £250, the total augmentation of capital during the half-year was only £85. 13s. 2d. It must be satisfactory to the shareholders to know that this expenditure was simply for rolling stock purchased some time previously upon deferred payments and there had been no expenditure upon capital account except for the payment of rolling stock. It showed that after discharging and setting aside the amount of money which was needed for the payment of debenture interest, there was a balance of £932 to credit upon the trading of the half-year and if they took the whole year, the revenue only fell short by £9.

Lucy regretted to say that the shipment of coal at Sharpness, notwithstanding the reduction in rates, had fallen off. The amount of tonnage leaving empty from Sharpness in 1883 was 318,074 tons, of that tonnage, 207,750 tons were too deep or too long to proceed to the present coal tip. Negotiations were now taking place in hope that some arrangement might be made by which another coal tip might be erected, thus taking full advantage of the available shipping.

He saw unmistakeable signs that they had passed the worst regarding the receipts, arrangements had been made with the Great Western Railway Company for the conveyance of South Wales steam coal to Southampton via the Severn Bridge route commencing on the previous 31 December, and he thought other merchandise must surely follow.

If he might state briefly what seemed to be needed, he would say it was unanimity; it was necessary for the shareholders to co-operate with the bond-holders. As they were aware, a committee of shareholders was appointed and they met the bond-holders at Lydney and although their questions departed from the instructions they were given at the meeting at which they were elected, they were met in a friendly spirit. But he was sorry to say they declined his invitation to inspect the whole of the railway and works and thus see the exact position in which their undertaking stood.

H. Bennett stated he was pleased to find the report of a more cheering character than it had been in recent years. He had been a member of the committee of shareholders, and referring to the erection of the new coal tip, he thought that this should be provided by the Dock Company and not by the Severn & Wye Section.

In referring to the accounts, he noticed that although the Company appeared to be doing fairly well, they were £947 short of paying their debts and £2,500 worse than they were the previous year. That being the state of affairs, it could not by any stretch of the imagination be said they were in a flourishing state (cries of 'Hear Hear'). They had, for the very first time been shown the earnings of each section during the half year. This information proclaimed the startling fact that while one section of the Company earned only eighteen and a half per cent it dipped its hands into the pockets of the shareholders and took thirty-one and a half per cent. While such a state of affairs continued, it could not be expected that there could be any unanimity of feeling, to which the chairman referred (cries of 'Hear Hear') and which all most ardently desired.

What the committee were anxious to bring about, was the abolition of the divided directorate and the division of interests amongst the shareholders and that the two Companies should amalgamate in the true sense and the whole concern should be subjected to re-organisation; such an arrangement was viewed as the only hope of success. He then proposed that 'in view of the present position of the Company, and in order to promote the future success and well being of the entire undertaking, the directors be respectfully requested and thereby instructed to prepare and lay before the shareholders at a special meeting to be convened for that purpose, at an early a date as possible, a scheme for the re-organisation and amalgamation of all the stocks and shares of the undertaking, so that the two sections may be fused into one company with the assistance of Parliament or other-wise.'

B.S. Stock seconded the motion and recorded his opinion of the injustice of the present arrangements. He stated the matter had been placed before the directors of the committee and they had met with a direct negative. But as long as the present system remained, so long would there be a divided board and hostility all round. They had begun last year with a debt owing from the Severn & Wye Section to the Bridge Section, of £2,200 which had now reached nearly £5,000, and he wondered if this kind of thing would ever be put right, or were they to be dragged deeper into the mud year by year, by a debt, which a false statement of the premises had created (Cries of 'Hear Hear').

Viner Ellis and J. Stanton added their contributions to the proceed-ings, agreeing with Bennet and Stock, but H. Waddy objected to the charges of unfairness and injustice which had been used and reminded the shareholders who opposed the existing arrangements, that they had been fully discussed before being agreed upon. C.H.S. Jones added an amendment to the Chairman's motion and proposed that the directors' report should be adopted with the omission of the paragraph 'In accordance with the report of the Engineer, the directors propose applying to the Court for permission to form a fund for the renewal of locomotives and other working stock'.

The amendment was carried by twenty-five votes to six. Lucy pointed out that no question of the amalgamation of capital could be dealt with until insuperable difficulties affecting the position of each bond-holder were settled. He agreed that such an amalgamation was needed, but the proposal was not a new one.

After some discussion, Bennett modified his proposal and submitted the following in its stead 'That the directors of this Company be requested to consider the desirability of re-arranging the capital of the Company so that the two sections of the joint section shall be completely fused into one undertaking.' The proposition was seconded and agreed upon. The meeting terminated with a vote of thanks from the chairman.

Thus ended another stormy meeting of the Severn & Wye and Severn Bridge Railway Company but in spite of the accusations, Lucy remained in full control of the situation. But other voices were now speaking out against the Company. At a meeting of the free miners at the Speech House on 12 April, W.B. Brain was given a warm reception. He drew attention to the want of proper railway facilities for travelling in and out and about the Forest. Acts of Parliament had been passed, some railraods had been constructed and one or two still remained closed. He had, on several occasions, discussed the matter with seven M.P.s. There was, at present, more coal than they knew what to do with and they badly needed better facilities for conveying it out of the Forest.

The Severn & Wye Section appeased

The case of the amalgamation came before Mr. Justice Chitty in the Chancery Division on Saturday 20 June 1885, upon a petition of the Company for its sanction to a scheme agreed to by more than the statutory numbers of persons interested.

The separate charges existing on the two companies were to be charged on the undertaking as a whole. After all outgoings had been paid, the balance was divided between two sections of the Company. In adjusting the accounts between the two sections, each section had to be charged with its own outgoings in respect to the debentures and mortgage charges on the undertaking. The amalgamation did not work, the Bridge Section did not pay and the Severn & Wye Section was earning eight per cent of the profits. The total income diminished and was only sufficient to pay the outgoing charges. Inasmuch as the Severn & Wye Section had charges to a larger extent, they found themselves continually in debt on account of the other sections, which caused dissatisfaction and disputes. Strikes in the districts surrounding the Railway prevented them paying their costs. From 1883 to 1885, the Company continued and £1,700 was received from the Company and was now deposited in the Court of Chancery. The order of 1883 which appointed the receiver and managers, also directed an account of the priority of the different charges. On that, several disputes arose and an attempt was made to get the numerous questions with regard to the priorities, settled by a special case. A very elaborate document, and some twenty-three counsel and solicitors met to settle the draft: the result, as might be expected, was a failure.

The parties then set to work to arrange a scheme for settling the disputes, and this scheme of arrangement eventually met with the approval of all the parties concerned.

The short effect of the scheme was that the secured creditors were to abate about £1,000 a year interest, all the debenture stocks to be consolidated, a new debenture stock issued at four per cent to be issued in lieu of the old and to be applied in paying off existing mortgage debts; one year's interest to be capitalised; the amount of the new debenture slightly to exceed the amount necessary for paying off the existing mortgage debts; all actions to be stopped; the guarantees given by the Midland Railway & Gloucester and Birmingham Navigation Company, for the debenture stock to be written off; the existing share capital to be converted into ordinary and preference shares to be called 'Preferencee "A", Preference "B", Preference "C" ' and Ordinary Stock, and to be apportioned among the shareholders according to their rights, a release of all claims by the two sections of the Company, the cancellation of the shares in the Bridge Section held by the Severn & Wye Section, the application of the income to paying the working expenses and rent charges, payment of the interest on the debenture and preference stocks; the receiver to be discharged from 31 December 1884 and the money in respect of the earnings of the Company for 1884 which may come to his hands in 1885, to go to the revenue account of the Company for 1885. The scheme was sanctioned by Mr. Justice Chitty.[o]

The amalgamation which had for so long bedevilled the Severn & Wye Section was now terminated, but an uneasy peace still prevailed.

The Company was now out of Chancery and great things were expected when Keeling, at a meeting of the Forest of Dean coal and iron traders, promised price reductions in freight to South Wales with more

92

concessions to follow.

In the doldrums

The seventeenth half-yearly meeting[11] was held at Bristol on 26 February 1888, and once again Lucy reported the Severn & Wye and Severn Bridge Railway Company in the doldrums. He said the directors regretted a falling off in receipts of £1,654 compared with the corresponding period of the previous year which mostly attributed to the state of the Forest coal trade.

The expenditure, however, was £2,203 less, mainly due to economy in maintenance and low charges. A further sum of £500 had been appropriated to the reserve fund for rolling stock and carried £68 14s. 2d., the balance of the net revenue account to the credit of the Preference "A" stock.

Keeling reported that the expenditure amounted to sixty-four per cent of the receipts. Dredging had been carried out at Lydney Canal and Docks but considerable inconvenience had been experienced during the past dry spell and steam pumps had been installed at the docks to maintain the water level, the water being drawn from the river when required. Only two and a half miles of track remained to be laid with steel rails and the Severn Bridge structure was in good order.

Tyers Electric Train Tablet Apparatus had been found to greatly facilitate the traffic between Lydney Town and Tufts Junction and its adoption was desirable as early as possible on other sections of single line where traffic was most frequent.

The meeting closed at the end of Keeling's report.

Once again The Severn & Wye and Severn Bridge Railway Company was at the mercy of the prevailing conditions in the Forest; the falling off of receipts being due to severe competition. The Forest coal owners had recently raised the price of coal by 1s. per ton, while in South Wales, the price had only been raised by 6d. per ton.

Gloom and despondency

The eighteenth half-yearly meeting[12] showed no improvement when Lucy announced that receipts were once again down, due to the depression of trade in the Forest and intense competition.

H. Bennett on hearing the report, said it seemed the heart had been taken out of the shareholders and they felt in a state of utter destitution. He did not desire to lose confidence in the directors, but he would urge them to relieve themselves of their burden in any way possible. He had thought, and in fact he mentioned on a former occasion, that the opening of the Severn Tunnel would very seriously affect the position of the Company. His remarks had been laughed at, but why he did not know, for they now found that a great deal of Forest coal was now despatched via the Severn Tunnel, although the natural outlet was the Severn Bridge.

Now they must wait for providence to turn something in their favour; it had been a source of great discouragement because there was great confidence in the undertaking by the older citizens of Bristol. He again urged the directors to take every step possible to recover their position.

H. Rake endorsed Bennett's remarks, and the chairman said the directors' task had for so long, been a disheartening one, they had emerged from one crisis, only to be overtaken by another.

Keeling presented the engineer's report, stating there had been a recent increase in Welsh and Forest coal to Sharpness. Painting of the Severn Bridge was now in progress and one of the swing bridge boilers had been repaired. Extensive repairs were also being carried out to the lock and harbour gates at Lydney. The Bicknor sidings and goods shed near Lydbrook were now open for traffic.

The meeting terminated with the usual thanks from Lucy

1890 *The twenty-second half-yearly meeting*

Lucy commenced the twenty-second half-yearly meeting[13] on Friday 22 August, on a cheerful note, when he told the assembled shareholders that the gross receipts had shown an increase of £806, and the directors recommended that a dividend at the rate of two per cent be paid on Preference "A" stock. He remarked that there was one item of traffic which he wished he could see more developed in the Forest, and that was iron ore, but he was afraid that this was now very unlikely owing to the introduction of Spanish ore and the manufacture of Bessemer steel.

With regard to their railway, it was now in a very efficient state, in fact more so than it ever had been since he had been connected with it.

The engineer reported that the re-arrangement and signalling of the transfer and marshalling sidings at Lydney Junction, had been completed and additional sidings and signals provided at Drybrook and Cinderford stations. One locomotive was being partially rebuilt at Bristol and a new one had been ordered from the Vulcan Foundry Company at Warrington.

Thus ended a very placid meeting of the Severn & Wye and Severn Bridge Railway Company.

A certain amount of modernisation had been carried out at Lydney, Drybrook and Cinderford, and such rare occasions as the payment of a

94

dividend was a forecast of brighter prospects for the Company. But before 1890 was over, the Forest was once again plunged into a series of disastrous strikes; by the middle of 1891, the distress in the Forest, was as bad as in the 1870s.

Stone breaking once again became the sole occupation of the miners; at a meeting at Coleford Police Court in May, Mr. Hawkins, the relieving officer, handed in an account of the work done in the first four days by the stone breakers. The rate of pay was 1s. per cubic yard, with an additional 2d. each for each dependent child, but in no case did the maximum earnings exceed 2s. per day. On one occasion, the most successful man had broken three-and-a-half cubic yards, for which he was paid 4s. 8d., one had achieved three and another two-and-a-half and it was at once evident that men would not work for such a pittance as this.

Altogether, twenty-two men, who between them had to support eighteen wives and seventy-six children, had earned by Saturday evening £2 16s. 8½d., an average of 6d. per week per mouth. Through the kindness of Mr. Nicholson, a supply of bread and cheese was distributed at the quarries, which helped a little, but even with this help, a man's earnings could hardly keep his family in bread alone.

On Thursday 6 May, a number of unemployed miners commenced work on the Coleford and Monmouth Railway at Coleford and early the next day a large number of men from Parkend, Yorkley, Pillowell and Whitecroft, arrived before 6.00a.m. but were unlucky in obtaining work. Many of these men had nothing to eat that day and nothing in the larder at home. Prospects in the Forest were again exceedingly bleak.

Bankruptcy threatens

On 31 July 1893 the following circular[13] was sent to the debenture holders of the Severn & Wye and Severn Bridge Railway Company.

> I am instructed to inform you that in consequence of the long and severe depression in the Forest coal trade which became acute during the past half year, the Company's revenue for that period proves insufficient for the discharge of the debenture interest. The prolonged labour difficulties in the Forest mining industry, which chiefly occasioned the depression referred to, have now resulted in the stoppage of the principal house coal collieries. An action has been taken against the Company by a holder of debenture stock preparatory to petitioning for the appointment of the directors as managers and the principal officers as receivers. Under the cir-

cumstances, the payment of interest must await the direction of the Court. You will readily appreciate the circumstances which have led to this result are entirely beyond the control of the Company, but it is hoped that the difficulties of the Forest district may soon be adjusted and the trade resume its normal condition. In this circular, it has been made abundantly clear that the Company is the victim of circumstances over which it has no control.

The periodic traffic returns have for months past shown a serious decrease in the revenue of the Company and the stoppage of the principal house coal collieries, owing to the still existing dispute between the coal owners and miners, has practically stopped the most important branch of the Company's traffic.

We understand the Company's business will proceed as usual and that when trade is restored to its normal condition by a settlement of the strike, the directors hope to be able to satisfy the claims of debenture holders, in which case, the Company would revert to the position it held prior to the present unfortunate difficulty. Interest on some of the debentures, it may be added, is guaranteed by other Companies.

The usual half-yearly meeting will shortly be held and the shareholders will then doubtless be informed as to the prsent financial position of the undertaking.

THOMAS LINTON
SECRETARY TO THE SEVERN & WYE AND
SEVERN BRIDGE RAILWAY CO., LYDNEY
31 JULY1893.

1894 At the crossroads

Once again the Company was in Chancery, Viner Ellis had obtained a judgment in respect of his unpaid debenture interest and the directors were appointed receivers.

The Midland Railway and Gloucester & Berkeley Navigation Companies were called upon to pay the interest on the £75,000 four per cent debenture stock issued under their guarantee.

During the last half year doubling of the line at Whitecroft and relaying work had been suspended, but essential work such as painting the Severn Bridge, repairs to the viaduct at Sharpness and improving the water supply to Lydney Locomotive sheds had continued. 4,500 tons of mud had also been dredged from Lydney Canal and a new house had been built for the Harbour Master.

The Severn & Wye and Severn Bridge Railway Company were now at

Sharpness New Docks 1875, opened in 1874.

Author's Collection

Modern Sharpness 1980, the low level swing bridge remains and the North side grass bank was replaced with a concrete quay wall by the Demolition and Construction Company in 1941.

R. Huxley

the crossroads, and the question foremost in everyone's minds was would the Company survive? Surely the directors and stockholders had had enough — the answer was not long in coming.

At a specially convened meeting[14] on 17 February, Lucy presented the shareholders with the details of the terms upon which Parliament would be asked to authorise the sale of the undertaking of the Severn & Wye and Severn Bridge Railway Company to the Midland Railway and Great Western Companies. He said the price to be paid for the railway had been fixed at £477,300, for which sum the purchasing companies would acquire an undertaking upon which £951,349 capital had been expended. The sum paid as the purchase price was to be distributed to the holders of Severn & Wye stock as follows:

To the registered proprietors of the £75,000, four per cent Guaranteed Debenture Stock, the sum of £125 for each £100.

To the holders of the £253,265, four per cent Debenture Stock, £100 for each £100 of stock.

Subject to the payment of all debts and liabilities, the surplus was to be divided as near as possible in the following proportions:

To the Proprietors of the £50,000 Preference "A" Stock, the sum of £57 for each £100 of that stock.

To the Proprietors of the £107,467 Preference "B" Stock, £29 for each £100 of stock.

To the Proprietors of the £298,269 Preference "C" four per cent £16 for each £100.

To the Proprietors of the £167,348 Ordinary Stock the sum of £12 for each £100 of stock.

The date from which the sale was to take effect was fixed from the coming 1 July, and it was further agreed between the purchasing companies that the Midland Railway should on payment of a sum agreed upon, or fixed by arbitration, transfer to the Great Western Railway half their interest in the Berkeley Branch Railway which should thence forward be worked by the two companies as part of the undertaking of the Severn & Wye and Severn Bridge Railway Company.

It was further agreed between the two companies that after the

Looking along the docks from the North Docks swing bridge; the Severn and Wye coal tip can be seen in the right background.

Author's Collection

Sharpness Docks with the 'Reigate Lyncor' in the foreground and the 'Penmound' of Falmouth behind.

Author's Collection

transfer of the Severn & Wye and Severn Bridge Railway Company, that that undertaking should be controlled by a joint committee of the two companies, to whom might also be delegated the powers and duties then exercised by the Great Western and Midland Consultation Committee, the Bristol Station Committee, the Clifton Extension Railway Joint Committee and the Halesowen Railway Joint Committee.

In detailing the circumstances leading up to the negotiations, Lucy pointed out that the directors had acted for what they believed to be in the best interests of the Company and in defence to the best wishes of the proprietors. The terms of the agreement were now completed and the purchase money was to be paid to the liquidators (who would be the then receivers, with an advising committee of directors, to save any charge for remuneration) on 2 July or as soon as possible after the Act was passed and within fourteen days of the appointment of the liquidators.

The Severn & Wye and Severn Bridge Railway Company were to realise their assets and discharge their liabilities and bear the expense of liquidation and of distributing the purchase money and by their directors and officers were to supply such evidence and assistance as they may be able to afford in promoting the application in Parliament to give effect to the arrangement, all other expenses in promoting the Bill and in relation to the sale, were to be born by the purchasing companies.

The directors were of the opinion that these terms embodied a fair and equitable division of the balance of the purchase money. The amounts at which the various classes were paid off would in every case, exceed the market value of the respective stocks for the period 1885 to 30 June 1893. During that period, preference "A" stock received intermittent dividends, the average over the whole term being one-and-one-eighth per cent per annum and the directors were of the opinion that no better average return could be looked for if the sale was not made.

With the exception of one dividend of three-eighths per cent on the preference "B" stock, there had been no return on the preference "B" and "C" and ordinary stock. The average net revenue during the same period amounted to £13,287, whereas if calculated upon the basis of investment in a high class trust security, the purchase money would represent an income of £14,557. After careful consideration, the directors believed there was a reasonable probability of the assets, after discharging all liabilities, being sufficient to meet the expense of the winding up, but the Bill provided that any deficiency should be met rateably by the various classes of preference and ordinary stocks and

The North Docks Branch swing bridge, the last remaining section of the Severn Bridge still in use, reconditioned and overhauled in 1980. The vessel on the left is the 'Wave' of the Gloucester and Sharpness Steam Packet Company who advertised and ran 'Delightful Water Cruises to Gloucester and Sharpness'. The Company ws founded by J.C. Francillon of Gloucester.

Author's Collection

The junction of the old and new docks, a side traversing coal tip is seen just in front of the vessels. Sharpness gas and dye works are also seen on the right hand side.

Author's Collection

these classes should participate in any surplus on a similar basis.

The directors from their knowledge of the position and prospects of the Company unanimously recommended to the proprietors to approve the Bill which would be submitted at the twenty-ninth half-yearly meeting to be held on the twenty-seventh of the month.

The twenty-ninth half-yearly meeting

The twenty-ninth half-yearly meeting[15] was held at the usual venue on 27 February. Lucy, in dealing with the accounts, said that there had been a considerable improvement in the coal trade since the previous September when the principal house coal collieries had resumed work. Expenditure had been a little higher, especially in the maintenance of the harbour and docks. However, he saw no reason why they should not make up the £600 arrears in the debenture interest and he trusted there might be a balance.

The chairman then proceeded to give the details of the sale of the railway and finally moved that the Bill for the sale of the railway be approved; the motion was seconded by J.A. Grahame Clarke, W. Giles (a shareholder) felt that the directors were deserving of a vote of thanks and gratitude of the proprietors for the satisfactory arrangements made for the sale of the undertaking. It was nice to know the line would still be worked for the benefit of the district and there was also further satisfaction that the shareholders were getting good value for their property. H. Bennett endorsed Giles' remarks; he felt the directors had done their utmost for the shareholders and were entitled to their thanks.

The resolution was moved and unanimously carried.

Lucy then referred to a circular sent out by G. White to the proprietors, asking them for their vote. He thought there were certain objectional clauses in it which if White had thought twice, he probably would not have used them. He felt it was unwise that shareholders should go about soliciting proxies when important issues were at stake, especially if they had any confidence in their directors, and in this case, he thought White had over-stepped the mark. George White, replying to the chairman's remarks, said if he had to write the circular over again, there was not one word he would alter. His holding in the Company was very large − £75,804 in the various classes of stock, and he had taken a great interest in the Company, but he was not prepared to place his interest in the hands of any board or body of gentlemen. He was, however, always ready to assist independent shareholders in any matters concerning the welfare of the undertaking. He felt the chair-

Sharpness Station, c. 1897.

Author's Collection

Sharpness Station, single lined in the 1950's and the station signal box removed. 6400 Class 0-6-0 T locomotive No. 6437 is seen auto working the Berkeley Road to Lydney Town passenger service.

F.C. Scoon

man, instead of lecturing him should have thanked him for his trouble taken on the subject. He then moved a vote of thanks to the directors for their part in the negotiations and this was seconded by H. Bennett. Lucy thanked the shareholders and said they were now all in complete agreement, that the course taken by the directors was the correct one. For the want of funds they had to cripple their railway, not forgetting the difficulties they had met in developing the Forest coal trade caused by the opposition of another Company, but he hoped the Midland Railway and Great Western Companies would do much to develop the trade of the district.

The death of G.B. Keeling

On 28 February, George Baker Keeling, who had been in ill health for some time, died at his home; Severn House, Lydney, in his eighty-first year.

He joined the Severn & Wye Railway and Canal Company in 1847 as secretary and general manager and acted in this capacity until 1879. He then became the managing director of the Severn & Wye and Severn Bridge Railway Company and remained so until the time of his death.

The funeral took place at St. Mary's Church, Lydney on Monday 25 March at 3.00p.m. and the service was conducted by the Reverend J.F.C. Bessant assisted by the Reverend R.M. Turner. Besides members of his family and friends, over 100 employees of the Severn & Wye and Severn Bridge Railway Company attended, which included station masters, plate layers, drivers and signalmen.

Objections to the sale

On Thursday 17 May it was rumoured that the Bill authorising the sale of the Severn & Wye and Severn Bridge Railway Company might be dropped in consequence of opposition by traders in the Forest of Dean. As a result, quotations on ordinary and preference stock declined on the Bristol Stock Market. Objections to the sale were coming from various companies and organisations. The Golden Valley Railway considered that the takeover would seriously hamper its plans for establishing a through route between the north and west of England, placing them in competition with the Midland Railway and Great Western Companies. The Golden Valley Railway obtained powers to run to Lydbrook in 1889 and already possessed running powers by which it joined the Cambrian system and then by the Wrexham and Ellesmere Railway, the Dee Bridge and the Mersey Tunnel Railway, therefore linking the Severn with Liverpool, with the Severn Bridge being a vital link on the route.

At a public meeting at Cinderford on 2 July, a local committee was elected to oppose the Bill, a report being prepared by Messrs. Robb and Dykins, indicated that the Midland Railway and Great Western could completely shut up the Forest if they so wished. Further objections were lodged regarding the high traffic rates and the fact that Cinderford Station was one-and-three-quarter miles from the town. The committee was asked to press for the opening of the Whimsey and Mitcheldean Railway.

The County Council was also not backward in promulgating their objections and resolved to oppose the Bill on the grounds that it would be injurious to the County as well as the Forest of Dean. They believed the Midland Railway and Great Western Railway were not interested in developing the Lydney and Sharpness Docks trade and they could also prevent the choice of routes.

Resolutions were passed that the maximum railway and terminal rates, short distance tolls, the Severn Bridge mileage, dock and harbour dues of the Severn & Wye and Severn Bridge Railway Company be revised. The two purchasing companies to complete and open for traffic certain lines authorised to be constructed by the Great Western Railway and provide in certain cases, better station facilities, also to open for traffic with proper connections to other lines, (The Whimsey and Mitcheldean Railway which belonged to the Great Western Railway had never been opened to traffic though the rails were laid), develop trade at Lydney and Sharpness and to effectively maintain and keep open Lydney Docks.

In July, the London and North Western Railway Company lodged a petition in the Private Bill Office of the House of Commons praying to be heard against the Bill for the transfer of the Severn & Wye and Severn Bridge Railway. In their petition, they set forth that they were at the present time, competitors with the Great Western Railway and Midland Railway for the traffic to and from places on the Severn & Wye and Severn Bridge Railway and they were apprehensive, that by means of the proposed amalgamation, it would be within the power of the Great Western Railway and Midland Railway to prevent traffic passing onto their system. They submitted that if the amalgamation took place, it should only be granted on the terms that their running power over the Severn Bridge be maintained.

Objections came from many quarters, but the Bill[16] received Royal Assent on 17 August and the undertaking became the joint property of the Midland Railway and Great Western Railway Companies and was named the Severn & Wye Joint Railway.

The Training Ship 'Vindicatrix' lies at its anchorage in the old Dock, in the right background can be seen the original Severn & Wye coal tip.

D. Knight

The final meeting

The thirtieth half-yearly meeting[17] was held on Thursday 23 August at the Royal Hotel, Bristol. W.C. Lucy presided, the notice convening the meeting was read by the secretary Thomas Linton and the report and accounts were taken as read.

Lucy, before proceeding, referred to the death of G.B. Keeling and regretted his passing. He then continued with the final business of the Company.

The receipts for the present half-year were £20,610 13s. 5d. against £17,504 for the previous half-year but the expenditure had increased by £461, which would naturally be accounted for in consequence of the increase in traffic. Only one item called for special notice and that was under the heading of rates and taxes for the existing year which was put down as £966. The rise was in consequence of revaluation of the East and West Dean districts, but a part would be refunded by the purchasing companies because the arrangements embraced after a time when they would have taken over the Company (1 July). The net results were these. They had paid off £604 the arrears of interest and added £110 to the reserve fund, and they had absorbed the whole of the receipts.

Taking all things into consideration, it was very satisfactory.

J. Press, a shareholder, enquired if they would be likely to receive the full amount of the £6,377 set down for general stores etc., and would there be a payment on account to the shareholders before the final distribution? Lucy replied that he could not say definitely regarding the £6,377 but hoped it would be very near that figure. They would also have to wait some time for final distribution, but in two months preference and ordinary shareholders would get a payment on account. Press asked the chairman if the Midland Railway and Great Western Railway companies would be willing to give shareholders the option of being paid in stock as they had to raise the money at three-and-a-half per cent to purchase the undertaking? Lucy thought this extremely unlikely.

An extraordinary meeting was then held for the purpose of appointing the liquidators. A remuneration of £100 was suggested for them, but Stewart Fripp moved that it should be altered to 100 guineas and Messrs. Lucy, Fripp, Keeling and Thomas Linton were appointed liquidators for winding up the affairs of the Company. Sir William Marling, Bart., moved a vote of thanks to Lucy for his long and valued service to the Company and the last meeting of the Severn & Wye and Severn Bridge Railway Company closed, to the echo of cheers from the shareholders. In fifteen years the Severn Bridge had bankrupted its owners and over ninety years later, was destined to bankrupt yet another company.

W.C. Lucy retires

Lucy fought long and hard to steer the Company on the road to financial success, but he had not bargained for the competition of the Severn Tunnel, and the unstable conditions in the Forest.

The avalanche of Welsh coal expected to find its way, by the cheaper route, over the bridge to London and other important markets never materialised in the quantities that Lucy expected, but he remained an optimist until the end.

The Great Western Railway Company, who had quietly encircled the Forest, maintained their stranglehold on the Severn & Wye and Severn Bridge Railway even though they were extremely unpopular in the area, and no doubt they laughed long and hard at the financial collapse of their competitor.

In 1894 a public subscription was organised by John Bellows of Gloucester to present Lucy with a portrait of himself. Lucy had resided in Gloucester for forty-four years and had been connected with the merchants of Gloucester for most of this period, as well as the Gloucester Banking Company, Sharpness New Dock Company and numerous other local organisations.

On 4 May 1895 Lucy was entertained to a dinner at the Guildhall and the mayor of Gloucester presented his portrait. Sufficient funds had been forthcoming to provide an illuminated album containing the names of the subscribers. The album bore the following inscription:— 'From Friends in the City and County of Gloucester who have presented William Charles Lucy, Esq. with his portrait and have provided a replica to be preserved in the City of Gloucester, 1895.' The portrait was painted by the Hon. John Collier.

Many glowing tributes were paid to Lucy who, shortly afterwards, slipped quietly into retirement.

Keeling involved at Newnham-on-Severn

In 1877 a scheme for bridging the river at Newnham[18] was dropped through lack of capital, the project was revived in 1880[19] but was again doomed to failure.

Fourteen years were to elapse before the idea was raised again. M.F. Carter of Newnham formed a committee with the Reverend Bevis, Rector of Arlingham, as his vice chairman, the venue chosen for their meetings was the Victoria Hotel.

Keeling and Reichenbach, who had been involved in the 1880 scheme, were again commissioned by the committee to survey the river on 7 April 1894, when float observations were conducted to determine the velocity of the tide. An engineering drawing[20] was produced for a bridge of eight spans, two of 285 feet, four of 121½ feet, one of 66 feet and one of 65 feet; the estimated cost being £25,000. The bridge was intended to cross from Church Road to the New Inn at Arlingham with a gradient of one in thirty-three up to Newnham.

Much was expected of the scheme and the County Council were approached in respect of financial support which, unfortunately, did not materialise.

This proved to be Keelings last major civil engineering project and one which should have proceeded further than the drawing board.

Keeling continued to work for the Joint Railway until his retirement early in the twentieth century; he spent his remaining years in Cheltenham until his death in 1913.

H.W. Paar in his *Severn Wye Railway* outlines Keeling's long and eventful career from which the Severn Bridge emerges as his greatest engineering triumph.

References to Chapter Five

1. *Gloucester Journal* 5 January 1880.
2. *Gloucester Journal* 22 February 1880.
3. *Gloucester Journal* 8 May 1880.
4. *Gloucester Journal* 25 February 1882.
5. *Gloucester Journal* 26 August 1882.
6. *Gloucester Journal* 23 December 1882.
7. *Gloucester Journal* 24 February 1883.
8. *Gloucester Journal* 25 August 1883.
9. *Gloucester Journal* 26 February 1884.
10. *Gloucester Journal* 27 June 1885.
11. *Gloucester Journal* 18 February 1888.
12. *Gloucester Journal* 18 August 1888.
13. *Gloucester Journal* 5 August 1893.
14. *Gloucester Journal* 24 February 1894.
15. *Gloucester Journal* 3 May 1894.
16. G.W. & M. (S. & W. & S.B.R.) Act 57 and 58 Vic., C.189.
17. *Gloucester Journal* 25 August 1894.
18. Gloucestershire Records Office. Engineering drawings Ref: Q. RUM.417.
19. Gloucestershire Records Office. Engineering drawings Ref: Q. RUM.432.
20. Gloucestershire Records Office. Engineering drawings Ref: Q. RUM.503.

CHAPTER SIX

Modernisation of the Severn Bridge

Weight restrictions applicable to steam
locomotives of the Western Region

With the possibility of a new marshalling yard being constructed at Brookthorpe, near Gloucester and with the occasional closure of the Severn Tunnel becoming more frequent for maintenance work, British Railways were investigating the possibility of more extensive use of the Severn Bridge route.

On the Western Region, routes are classified by a colour code and each class of locomotive displays a coloured disc indicating the route over which it may operate. Examples of the colour code are:–

Colour	Class of Locomotive
Double Red	4–6–0 King Class
Red	4–6–0 County, Hall Castle and Grange Class
Blue	4–6–0 Manor Class, 2–8–0 28xx
Blue	2–6–0 63xx
Yellow	0–6–0 22xx; 0–6–0T 57xx; 2–6–2 45xx; 4–4–0 90xx
All routes	0–6–0 16xx; 0–6–0 20xx; 0–6–0T 54xx

Therefore, a Double Red Locomotive may work over double red routes only, a red locomotive over double red and red routes only, a blue locomotive over double red, red and blue routes and a yellow locomotive over all routes. During a year, a number of 2–6–0 63xx locomotive classified blue, made a number of crossings of the bridge with special permission being granted for each, the occasions being usually at the weekend when the Severn Tunnel was closed to traffic for maintenance, a practice which had been in operation since 1923.

Prior to nationalisation, the Great Western Railway had, on numerous occasions, attempted to remove the weight restrictions from the bridge, but the London, Midland & Scottish Railway Company who were responsible for its maintenance frowned upon their efforts. In 1932, a scheme was proposed to raise the decking of the bridge to rail level and use the bridge for road as well as rail traffic. The idea was again mooted at the outbreak of the war in 1939, but finally abandoned owing to the problem of controlling mixed traffic and the hazards of cross winds.

The permitted loading across the Severn Bridge was 'Yellow Locomotives' with special permission for Blue Locomotives except 28xx Class. It was considered advantageous to increase this loading to 'Red Locomotives'. Existing calculations indicated that the bridge could carry Red Locomotives at a speed of three revolutions per second without any strengthing to the girder work. The chief civil engineer, Western Region, however, considered it desirable to verify the figures obtained. At his request, the research department of British Transport Commission attached electric resistance strain gauges at selected points and recorded the changes in strain during the passage of a test train.

A detailed examination of the Severn Bridge was completed in 1955 and the under line bridges. Numbers 3, 6, 11, 23, 27 and 35 between Berkeley Road and Lydney Junction were also subjected to a thorough inspection during the same period. Numbers 3 and 11 were considered defective inasmuch as they would be over-stressed by the passage of heavy locomotives, and it was recommended that the longitudinal troughs be reconstructed.

Preparations for the tests

On Wednesday 18 April 1956, Messrs. Lucas and Newsham of British Transport Commission research department, Derby arrived at Sharpness for an on-site meeting to discuss the preparations for the load tests. They were met by Messrs. Thompson, Edwards, Stone and Phelps of the district civil engineer's office, Gloucester and chief civil engineer's steel works section and it was decided that as the bridge painting would commence at the following Whitsun, the painters would be in a position to assist in erecting scaffolding when and where it was required.

Thompson and Edwards were left with the final arrangements regarding the test train consisting of two Castle class locomotives with a train of 8 × 20 ton capacity Grampus mineral wagons loaded with one-and-a-quarter to one inch ballast, with a brake van. During the weeks preceding the tests, the work of the attaching of the strain gauges to the bridge structure proceeded at a steady rate, not an easy operation when faced with removing several layers of paint from the bridge structure and preparing a smooth surface on the exposed metal.

The strain gauge recording equipment and portable power supply was installed in one of the shelters formed by the finials at the Lydney

111

end, and a duplicate system was provided at the swing bridge end to avoid long cable runs.

A total of fifty-seven electrical resistancee strain gauges were attached to three spans of the bridge, nineteen on the 134 foot span at the Lydney end, twenty on the adjoining 312 foot span and eighteen on the swinging span at the Sharpness end.

The gauges were distributed between the top and bottom chords and the vertical and diagonal members of the bracings. In addition, a gauge was attached to the web of the centre cross girder and two to floor plates onthe 134 foot span, and to the web and flange of the centre cross girder.

The final dates for the tests were scheduled for 15 and 22 July 1956, and special instructions were issued to the locomotive drivers for the occasion. 'Under no circumstances are the two locomotives to be allowed to proceed into the station loop at Sharpness or proceed into the North Docks branch. Sufficient water to be taken on at Lydney for the day's operations. The test train must be propelled tender first over the Bridge.'

On Sunday 15 July, numbers 5018 St. Mawes Castle, driver, J. Merrett and fireman K. Gough, and 5042 Winchester Castle, driver V. Whitcombe, and fireman T. Bartlett, left Gloucester motive power depot for Lydney to conduct the heaviest load test in the bridge since 3 and 4 October 1879. The test train was coupled up at Lydney and arrived at the bridge shortly after 8.00a.m. making a total load of approximately 480 tons.

Several runs at five miles per hour were made on the 312 foot span until recordings had been taken from all the strain gauges. A deflection of one-and-a-half inches was measured on the 312 foot span. Recordings were then made on the 134 foot span using the locomotives coupled together, minus the test train.

On 22 July the swing bridge span was similarly tested, using the same two locomotives coupled together. During this test, the swing bridge was opened to allow the passage of a ship along the canal and the opportunity was taken of recording the stress changes on the gauges, which at the time were in use.

From a preliminary analysis of the recordings taken during the test, it was seen that on 15 July, the gauges on the diagonals of the 134 foot span were not functioning correctly. Therefore, on 1 August, a further series of test runs were carried out. On this occasion, only one Castle, number 5018, was available and the tests were conducted on a between trains occupation.

15th July, 1956. 5018 St. Mawes Castle, and 5042 Winchester Castle stand on the first 134 foot span, a combined weight of over 250 tons during the load tests on the bridge.
Chief Civil Engineer, British Rail, Paddington

Conclusions (test report E140)

Calculations were made predicting the mean stresses set up by the passage of the test train and the preliminary examination of the test data showed that the measured values for the bottom trusses were lower than the calculated values, and in the case of the top chords, the measured values were closer to the calculated ones and, in some cases, were slightly higher.

The greatest range of stress recorded was on the 134 foot span in a diagonal member of the bracing, where the stress varied between 7.1 tons per square inch in tension and 4.6 tons per square inch compression, measured from the unloaded condition.

During the passage of the test train it was noticed that the diagonals vibrated, giving rise to alternating stresses varying in magnitude up to approximately ± 1.5 tons per square inch, therefore the question of fatigue was considered.

Although the stresses measured in the bridge were generally low, the possibility existed that the high stress in the diagonals in conjunction with the vibrations would prohibit the use of Castle class locomotives.

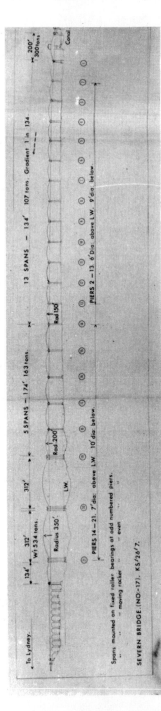

An engineering drawing of the bridge.

District Civil Engineer, British Rail, Gloucester

A theoretical study of this problem was made with the object of determining the possible future life of the diagonals if Castle class locomotives were permitted to use the bridge. The following assumptions were made:

1.   That the only mode of failure to be feared was that of fatigue.

2.   That the range of stress recorded in a member during a loading cycle should be the value considered in assessing fatigue life.

3.   That the wrought iron, of which the bridge was made was similar in fatigue properties to the wrought iron used in Gloucester Over Bridge then dismantled, and the Old Clyde Bridge, Glasgow, both of which belonged to the same era as the Severn Bridge.

It was necessary to make an estimate of the fatigue limit of the wrought iron of the bridge and for this purpose, the results of fluctuating tension tests on wrought iron specimens cut from Over Junction Bridge and the Old Clyde Bridge were used. The results of test specimens containing a rivet hole were pooled and gave a fatigue limit stress range of 7 tons per square inch, which made it possible to ignore the vibration component of 1.5 tons per square inch in the 312 foot span. The fatigue results available were used to calculate the endurance for 0.5 and 0.01 probabilities of failure (i.e. 1 in 2 and 1 in 100) at three stress range levels, eight, eleven and thirteen tons per square inch.

From the preparatory work at Sharpness, an estimate had been made of the numbers and types of locomotives crossing the bridge during a week, and these figures are shown in the following table, the locomotives and tender weights being given as fractions of the weight of a Castle class:

Locomotive type	Relative weight	Frequency of crossings per year
Castle class	1.00	?
2–6–0, 63xx	0.80	50
0–6–0, 2251	0.63	200
0–6–OT 16xx	0.39	700
0–6–OT, 20xx	0.29	1,300
0–4–2T, 48xx	0.33	3,000

Since there was a speed restriction of fifteen miles per hour over the bridge, it was assumed that there was no dynamic suggestion of the stresses produced. The stress in any diagonal was therefore approximately proportional to the weight of the locomotive pasing and since stresses had been measured for a Castle class locomotive, those due to other types could be readily calculated.

It was therefore possible to construct another table of stress and frequency, using as a basis, the worst case recorded, that is the stress range of 11.7 tons per square inch in a diagonal of the 134 foot span. This figure had been rounded to 12.0 tons per square inch in the calculation.

Locomotive Type	Stress Range tons per square inch	Frequency of crossings per year
Castle	12	?
2–6–0, 63xx	9.6	50
0–6–0, 2251	7.6	200
0–6–0T, 16xx	4.7	700
0–6–0T, 20xx	3.5	1,300
0–4–2T, 48xx	4.0	3,000

From the cumulative damage aspect only, the stresses above the fatique limit were taken into account. Thus all stresses of 7.0 tons per square inch and below were considered as making no contribution to cumulative damage. From a graph of the fluctuating tension tests, the endurance of wrought iron at 9.6 tons per square inch was 43,000 cycles and at 7.6 tons per square inch was 230,000 cycles for 0.01 probability of failure. If it was assumed that the locomotives (2–6–0 and 0–6–0) producing those stresses had been running over the bridge since they had been built forty-five and twenty-five years previously, then their respective contributions were $\frac{2250}{43000}$ and $\frac{5000}{230000}$ that was, 0.052 and 0.022. Assuming that these two locomotives, the 2–6–0 and 0–6–0 continued to use the bridge for a further ten years, their future share of the bridge life would be $\frac{500}{43000}$ and $\frac{2000}{230000}$ i.e. 0.012 and 0.009. Thus, at the end of ten years, the life expended would be obtained by the addition of the fractions obtained $0.052 + 0.012 + 0.009 = 0.095$. For stresses of twelve tons per square inch due to the Castle class locomotives the expectancy of life for 0.01 probability of failure from a graph was 5,800 cycles. However, 0.095 of the total life had already been assigned and from the calculations the expectancy of life at twelve tons per square inch, was reduced to 2,930 cycles.

The frequency at which it was proposed to run Castle class locomotives was not known but at four per week, the life for the bracings would be therefore, approximately fourteen years. Consideration was given to accuracy of this argument on fatigue and so the possible sources of errors were listed.

There was no direct evidence that the fatigue properties of the wrought iron of the Severn Bridge were the same as those based on the results of tests on specimens from the material from the other two bridges.

However, the tested material was of poor quality and it was unlikely that the Severn Bridge wrought iron was worse. In addition, the test specimen contained a rivet hole, a condition which was representative of the structure except that the rivet holes in the specimen did not contain rivets.

The stress history of the bridge was estimated on the basis of casual observation during the summer of 1956 and the assumption that the loadings had been similar for the previous large number of years considered was an obvious source of inaccuracy. On the other hand, it was reasonable to think that as locomotive weights had increased, the estimate would be a safe one although it was possible that other locomotives than ex-Great Western Railway once used the bridge during the time operation was not in Great Western Railway or Western Region hands.

Although the remaining life of the bracings calculated did not seem to be adequate, it was remembered that for the periods of life stated, the probability of failure was only 1 in 100, therefore it would be expected that in the time stated, only one bracing member in approximately three spans would fail.

As the bridge was a highly redundant structure, the failure of one diagonal would not have dangerous consequences and so, provided that regular and thorough inspection of the bridge was maintained, a very limited use by Castle class locomotives might be permitted.[1]

Modifications

As a result of the tests, a decision was made to strengthen the diagonal bracings throughout the bridge to eliminate the high secondary stresses which were found to occur in the members – modifications which were considered inevitable if the bridge was to be kept in service beyond 1970. Prior to inviting tenders to contract for the project, British Railways had investigated the possibility of utilising their own labour force, but the shortage of skilled steel erectors finally settled the issue.

Tenders were received from P.W. Maclellen Ltd., London; Fairfield Bridge and Shipbuilding Co., Chepstow; Horseley Bridges & Thos. Piggot, Staffs. and Joseph Westwood & Co. Ltd., London. The contract consisted of replacing 488 diagonals on all spans of the bridge except the swing bridge using approximately 50,000 bolts in the process. The contract was won by Fairfields, the price being fixed at £95,000 and other work taken up by them consisting of repairs to the piers in the form of banding and repairs to some of the expansion rollers which had become misaligned.

Early in 1960, work on the bridge commenced at the Lydney end, the bridge being open to contractors after the passage of the 9.45p.m. "H" Lydney to Stoke Gifford train, which was at approximately 10.00a.m. on the bridge.

A temporary hand operated siding was provided at Severn Bridge Station which was clipped, spiked and padlocked during normal hours and at Sharpness, a stop block was provided, adjacent to Pier 1, after the passage of the last train.

By the end of September, the first small span and the two 312 foot spans had been modified and the scaffolding erected on span eighteen which was well into the process of modification by 25 October.

References to Chapter Six

1. British Transport Commission, British Rail Division, Research Department.
    Report No. E140 "Stresses in Bridges, Tests on the River Severn Bridge at Sharpness, Gloucestershire."
    Authors C.B. Pennington and R. Newsham
    and the kind permission of R.W. Sparrow, deputy director of laboratories (engineering) and F.R.L. Barnwell, C.C. engineer, British Rail, Western Region.

CHAPTER SEVEN

The End of the Line

The tanker accident

Throughout the years the Severn Bridge had been the scene of numerous accidents involving ships navigating the river.

The trow *Brothers* thirty-nine tons, was wrecked and lost in a collision with one of the piers in 1879 and the *Victoria* employed during the construction work was wrecked in the 1880s.

One of the worst accidents took place in 1938[1] when a tug towing three tanker barges, the *Severn Pioneer, Severn Traveller* and *Severn Carrier* arrived at Sharpness very early on the evening tide. The barges were caught broadside by the fast flowing currents and swept into the bridge near the east bank. The hawser connecting the barges became wrapped round one of the piers and the vessels capsized, several men were drowned and the body of one was never recovered.

As a result of the accident the bridge was closed to traffic for twenty-four hours for inspection and subsequently re-opened when it was learned that it had suffered no apparent damage.

Later, an enquiry was held into the cause of the accident, and it was established that the crews, anxious to be home early that evening, had arrived too early on the flood tide, the normal practice being to arrive near the top of the tide when the initial rush of the currents had subsided. The old proverb 'More haste, less speed' had held true with fatal results.

During the Second World War, the Luftwaffe paid numerous visits to the area and in 1941 a near miss was recorded when a bomb fell on the road near Purton Manor. Perhaps one of the greatest threats to the bridge came not from the enemy, but from the Royal Air Force, when many pilots thought it a great thrill to fly beneath the 312 foot spans, and one memorable occasion a Vickers Wellington was observed to pass sedately beneath the bridge.

Following numerous complaints a small detachment of R.A.F. police were sent to investigate and were billeted at the Severn Bridge Hotel. From the maintenance hut near the viaduct, overlooking the mudflats, they maintained a vigil on the offenders, aircraft numbers were recorded and a few courts martial saw an abrupt cessation of the 'buzzing' of the bridge.

The next accident was destined to take place in the age of modern navigation aids, and proved to be an accident of catastrophic proportions which eventually set seal on the fate of the bridge.

The night of 25 October 1960 is one that will be long remembered by the inhabitants of both sides of the river near the Severn Bridge.

High water that evening was at 11.15p.m., and at 10.00p.m. a number of tankers were proceeding upstream to Sharpness. Among them were the M.V.'s *Arkendale H* and *Wastdale H.* All the vessels had encountered fog patches in the lower reaches of the Severn, but off Berkeley Nuclear Power Station (then under construction), the fog was quite dense.

In the meantime, T.C. Francis, New Works Inspector, had left the signal box at Severn Bridge station at 10.30p.m. after collecting the keys for the night occupation on the bridge. He noted that the night was dull with a fairly thick fog on the river, but above the fog, he could see the navigation lights on the bridge and the lights of Sharpness. As he walked along the 'up' platform, he could hear the tide roaring in the region of the bridge. Suddenly, he saw a sheet of red flame leap into the air, higher than the bridge, followed by the sharp sound of an explosion. The flames and explosion seemed to be on the down stream side of the bridge, and was followed by a low roar for a few seconds, followed by silence.

Francis dashed onto the bridge and saw two tankers burning and he immediately raced to the signal box to telephone for the ambulance and notify the police. He then returned to the bridge and found that part of the bridge and track had vanished and the cables torn away. On arrival at span eighteen, he was shocked to see the next two spans had gone, having not heard any sound of them hitting the water. By this time the tankers were burning fiercely and were aground on the upstream side of the bridge.

Captain G. Thompson, the skipper of the *Arkendale*, later in the night gave a dramatic account of how his vessel became lost when he found he was near the old entrance to Sharpness docks. Suddenly the *Wastdale* was alongside his vessel and there was a collision. The two vessels were held together by suction and were out of control. The tide then still running fast, swept the helpless tankers onto the bridge, the *Wastdale* striking the pier first.

The river was a mass of flames and Thompson swam to the shore near Lydney. But in the holocaust, H.J. Dudfield, A. Bullock, M. Hart, P. Simmonds and R. Niblett, lost their lives. Eye witnesses still recall the night of horror and how they were powerless to assist, as the luckless

120

members of the crews were swept away.

At dawn next day, the full extent of the damage was known. Pier seventeen and two spans had disappeared into the channel without trace, the gas main from Sharpness to Lydney which was installed in 1954, was severed and many homes in Lydney were without breakfast that morning. The G.P.O. communications via the bridge were also disrupted.

The same morning, the Lydney-Sharpness train ran via Gloucester and was worked that day only by locomotive 44167, 0–6–0, the crew having an uncomfortable time as it travelled tender first.

Later in the day, the two tankers (aground between Purton on the east bank and Sharpness) were blasted open by high explosives and allowed to settle into the sand, where they are still visible today.

On 27 October the Berkeley Road to Sharpness branch was auto worked connecting with the existing main line service which continued until 7 September 1964 when the branch was closed to passenger services.

Work was started almost immediately on a temporary gas supply for Lydney, where emergency services were provided by installing gas cylinders in the homes of those affected and eventually the normal supply over the bridge was restored on 8 November, being engineered by the Cleveland Bridge and Engineering Company and William Press Ltd. The gap in the gas pipeline was completed with a plastic hose, which was later dismantled and the supply re-routed further up the river.

Restoration of the Severn Bridge

During November, the chief civil engineer's department, Western Region, British Railways had provided drawings for the restoration of the bridge, with estimates of the cost. The new bridge section was designed to bridge the whole gap, fabricated from mild steel and welded, the total weight 350 tons, estimated cost £85,000, removal and re-building pier sixteen, £22,500; removal of pier seventeen, dredging 200 tons of 'pitching', building coffer dam, erecting new pier composed of concrete cylinders with a solid top, £40,000; provision of track between piers sixteen and twenty inclusive; £4,000. Engines, lighting, cranes etc., £22,000; piling forty-five feet long for coffer dam etc., £14,500.

The method considered for erecting the span, was described in the *Journal of the Institute of Civil Engineers*, November 1947 entitled "End on launching of trusses at close centres on rollers."

121

At Sharpness investigations had been carried out concerning details of land readily available to contractors. It was found that land near the swing bridge (Hamiltons old site) was available, also at the North Dock Branch Sidings, and at the South side of the main dock basin.

A survey of the damage

Early in December 1961, the *M.V. Universal Dipper* owned by Universal Divers Ltd., of Liverpool, carried out an extensive underwater survey in the region of piers sixteen, seventeen and eighteen. The vessel carried a crew of six, including divers and was also equipped with echo sounding apparatus.

The survey was completed in a month prior to which it was decided to erect a temporary trestle under the bridge adjacent to pier sixteen which was extensively damaged and leaning slightly towards the Sharpness bank. Several firms were invited to tender and a special clause reminded the firms to take into consideration the tidal characteristics of the River Severn. A formal order for the contract was given to Peter Lind & Co. Ltd., to commence work on 31 January. The contract was considered to be the first stage of the reconstruction of the bridge.

More damage to the bridge

The twin floating crane *Tweedledum and Tweedledee* hired by Peter Lind and Company at a cost of £375 per week of forty-four hours, was brought from Liverpool but was delayed by gales in the Irish Sea. Eventually, the twin craft arrived at the bridge on 22 February, but leaks were found in the hulls and repairs were effected, causing inevitable delays. On 17 February, the bridge sustained further damage when the tanker *B.P. Explorer* capsized on the way up to Sharpness. It drifted out of control upstream and struck pier twenty when drifting downstream on the receding tide. On the next tide, the tanker drifted upstream, finally becoming stranded on a sandbank at Awre. Damage to the bridge was estimated at £12,740. The entire crew were drowned, and the mystery of how it capsized was never fully explained.

A further day of drama on the Severn, took place on 14 April, when the *Tweedledum and Tweedledee* broke away on the flood tide. The event was witnessed by Driver W. Hardy (on special leave from British Transport Commission and acting as river adviser to Peter Lind & Company); and A.H. Cole, permanent way ganger of Blakeney, and Mr. Woodward, a fisherman.

Hardy raised the alarm at Sharpness and boarded the *M.V. Magpie* later picking up Cole on the opposite shore. Several attempts were made to take the twin craft in tow, and finally the *Magpie's* propellor was fouled by a rope.

The twin craft then drifted downstream from Awre, striking the dolphins on pier twenty and the jib striking the underside of the bridge, finally running aground off Lydney. Damage to the dolphins was estimated at £6,000.

Truly it seems, as Shakespeare wrote, 'When sorrows come, they come not single spies, but in battalions.'

The *Tweedledum and Tweedledee* was repaired at Avonmouth and arrived back on station on 7 May, an emergency procedure was adopted and new moorings laid, but the contract should have been completed by 2 May.

In recognition of their efforts, Driver Hardy and Ganger Cole were presented with monetary awards at Severn Bridge Station on Thursday 29 June by F.R.L. Barnwell, the Chief Civil Engineer, Western Region, British Railways.

High Court action

During 1961, the case between John Harker Ltd. and British Transport Commission, The Fairfield Shipbuilding and Engineering Company Ltd., South West Gas Board and the Postmaster General came before the High Court of Justice, Admiralty Division.

Fairfield's claim was that in consequence of the collision, they had lost plant, gear, tools and other materials. As a result of this they had also incurred additional transport and other costs because of the loss of access to the bridge at the Lydney end, which involved travelling via Gloucester to Sharpness to complete their contract.

The sum claimed by Fairfields was £8,704 10s. 8d. detailed as follows:—

> Plant and tools £1,888 12s. 3d., scaffolding materials, the property of Scaffolding (G.B.) Ltd., Sub-contractors and other costs incurred restarting the contract £3,070 18s. 3d., extra costs in transport to Sharpness £3,272 0s. 4d. Miscellaneous costs, £378 17s. 5d., Salvage Association's fee and charges £28 18s. 3d., Agency £26 5s. 0d.

But when the proceedings terminated British Rail was awarded £5,000 and Fairfields Shipbuilding & Engineering Company Ltd., a little over £100.

The 'Arkendale H' and 'Wastdale H' on the Ridge sandbank; their hulks can still be seen over twenty years after the accident.

Chief Civil Engineer, British Rail, Paddington

The future of the bridge in doubt

In April 1962 the possibility of reconstructing the bridge was still being actively pursued, several contractors being considered. Dorman and Long were expected to sub-contract for the supply of materials and the other companies considered were John Howard & Company Limited, Cleveland Bridge Engineering Company Limited, Peter Lind and Company Limited, and Sir William Arrol & Company Limited. The estimated cost was now £300,000 plus £600 for repairs to pier twenty.

Many local newspapers had reported that British Railways were abandoning the railway, owing to the high cost of repairs, but a spokesman in London informed the interested parties that a definite decision had not been made and plans were being constantly reviewed.

It was also rumoured that legal action was contemplated by a person residing in the Sharpness area against British Railways for failing to provide a passage across the river, his contention being that a clause in the Severn Bridge Railway Act ensured that a passage should be maintained by the concern that superseded the Purton Passage Ferry. As no such clause existed, the matter was not pursued.

124

26th October 1960, the morning after the accident. Fairfields working party on the night of the 25th opted to take an early meal break to listen to the Henry Cooper v Karl Muller boxing match on the radio at Severn Bridge Station, had they continued to work normally the death toll would have reached catastrophic proportions.

Chief Civil Engineer, British Rail, Paddington

The redundant asset

For several years following the tanker accident, much speculation took place regarding the future of the Severn Railway Bridge. Local councils on both sides of the river had, on more than one occasion, placed the matter high on their agenda.

The cost of repairs would be extremely high, in the region of £300,000 and British Railways had already investigated the possibilities of alternative routes which were now in full operation, the only hardship incurred by rail travellers, being on the occasions when the Severn Tunnel was closed for maintenance, which involved the long

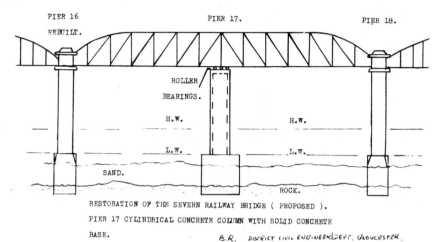

PIER 16 REBUILT.   PIER 17.   PIER 18.

ROLLER
BEARINGS.
H.W.   H.W.
L.W.   L.W.
SAND.
ROCK.

RESTORATION OF THE SEVERN RAILWAY BRIDGE (PROPOSED).
PIER 17 CYLINDRICAL CONCRETE COLUMN WITH SOLID CONCRETE
BASE.   B.R, DISTRICT CIVIL ENGINEERS DEPT, GLOUCESTER.

British Rail's drawing, produced within a month of the tanker accident gives details of
the proposed restoration of the Severn Bridge.

detour via Gloucester, adding approximately an hour for the journey.

In 1963, negotiations were in hand for the disposal of the bridge to
the Central Electricity Generating Board for use as a transmission line
crossing. A Bill to authorise the transfer of the bridge to the Board was
to be submitted to Parliament in June 1964, but in December it was
learned that they were no longer interested.

Demolition had been considered in 1960, but this was not taken up
owing to the high cost, and the position had been left for five years,
subject to further review at the end of that period. Now the only
alternative left was demolition.

On Tuesday 13 July 1965, F.R.L. Barnwell, Chief Civil Engineer,
Western Region, arrived at Sharpness, with a party of Army demolition
experts to discuss the project. Amongst the party were Brigadier R.L.
France, chief engineer, H.Q. Western Command; Major Jay, H.Q. 43
Division Engineers, Southern Command; Colonel Gordon, comman-
ding officer, 23 Group, Hereford; Major Nottingham, explosives expert
and Major Wilkinson and Lieutenant Colonel Smeadon, Local Territo-
rial Army Groups.

After some discussion, Brigadier France asked for detail drawings of
the bridge trusses, deck construction and river bed and rock levels for
further investigations. But eventually plans for a military exercise in
demolition was dropped for various reasons, one being the question of
liability.

British Railways had, in the meantime, discovered the possibility of disposal of the bridge spans as building units, with a possible profit from the sales and demolition would now be carried out with this end in view.

Demolition

Under the heading of 'Recovery and Disposal of Redundant Assets', tenders for the demolition of the bridge were sent to twenty-four firms. tenders to be returned by 20 April 1965.

Amongst the firms considered were Derek Crouch (Contractors) Limited; Underwater Welders Limited, Cardiff; Demolition & Construction Company Limited, London; I.P.L. Shipyards of Sharpness and Fairfields, Shipbuilding & Engineering Company Limited. On Thursday and Friday 3 and 4 March, inspection meetings for the prospective contractors were held at Severn Bridge station at 10.30a.m. with continuation meetings held in the afternoon at 2.30p.m. After hearing the magnitude of the project, twenty of the twenty-four firms invited to tender, quickly withdrew, one firm quoted £750,000 and another approximately £200,000, while the estimated price of a third was in the region of £80,000.

The contract for demolition was won by H. Morgan of the Nordman Construction Company Limited, Gloucester. Although not invited to tender originally, their tender was accepted as the cheapest.

The minimum amount of third party insurance cover for the project, was £250,000, the contract insisted that the entire structure be removed, all piers and foundations to be removed to river bed level, military trestling be removed and reclaimed for British Railways use. The viaduct adjacent to Severn Bridge station to be raised to the ground and removed.

The contractor to consult and make arrangements with all interested authorities including British Waterways, in respect of the swing bridge. If and when it was anticipated that explosive charges would be used the coastal authorities and the Severn Wildfowl Trust were to be informed and consulted. These items were discussed at a meeting with Nordman Construction Company on 19 October 1965, when H. Morgan was asked to provide a working schedule of the forthcoming operation, bearing in mind that the County Planning Officer would press for the complete removal of all the features previously mentioned.

The contractor's method

Early in 1967, Nordman Construction Company in a statement to the press[2], announced that work would soon be commencing on the demolition of the Severn Bridge; the whole operation would be completed in approximately five months, during which time firms from various parts of the country would be coming to the banks of the Severn to witness the Company's methods of demolition, a team of sixty highly skilled steel erectors would be engaged and sightseers would not be allowed within a mile of the bridge.

   J. Tyrer, the district civil engineer, British Rail, Gloucester; received Nordman Construction Company's demolition plan and schedule in June, which is outlined below:

Phase One

Floating crane *Magnus II* will be used to lift all spans of the bridge including the swing bridge. Attaching of slings and cables, hoisting, underwater cutting and general handling of spans from the bridge to the shore will be carried out by Ulrich Harms men (the owners of *Magnus II.*) Removal of rails, ties, cutting of anchor bolts, handling of spans and cutting on the shore to be handled by Nordman Construction Company's labour. This applies to concrete filled C.I. piers.

1.   Make swing bridge operable, request assistance from
     British Railways Swindon to instruct our operator.

2.   Remove track and sleepers.

3.   Remove gas main.

4.   Cut anchor bolts.

5.   Construct rail track along west shore to transport
     metal from cutters to viaduct hoist.

6.   Floating crane to move in 1–5 August 1967.

7.   Prepare to lift off span 15–16, 163 tons, a special cradle to be
     constructed for each lifting point position approximately 30 feet
     off centre and immediately adjacent to the nearest cross member.
     All points of lift will be accurately set out in order that cables to
     not foul the span. The crane's chains or slings will be attached
     during a rising tide and lift off will take place during high water.
     The spans' will be prevented from swinging by guide lines
     attached to the crane's capstans. The span will be then deposited
     on the west shore south of the bridge for cutting.

8.   After removing span 15–16, the crane will take the weight of the
     military trestling while divers will cut trestles under water and

The tanker 'BP Explorer', wrecked in the river with all hands lost, seen during salvage work at Awre in 1961. The tanker was repaired but later lost at Barry, South Wales.

R. Huxley

The summer of 1964 saw the last passenger carrying train arrive at Severn Bridge (for Blakeney) Station. A rail tour by the Railway Enthusiasts Club travelled over the whole of the Forest railway network for the last time.

D. Knight

the whole structure deposited on west shore, weight of structure, 60 tons approximately.

9. The remaining spans east of the break will be removed as per paragraph 7, but subsequent removal will be dependent on tidal conditions. The crane will be working 24 hours per day and therefore will have the advantage of two tides. At high water, work will continue on spans over deeper water. Span 14–15, 107 tons will be tested for rigidity and stability during lift off and if successful, will be deposited on Sharpness Quay. If unsuccessful, it will be deposited on the west shore. This lift will determine the fate of the small spans, for if successful, 12 will be shipped overseas, otherwise spans will be scrapped on west shore.

10. When all the bridge spans or span 1–2, have been removed, masonry pier 1 will be demolished and debris spread along the bank. This will allow the crane to float in and attempt to lift off the swing bridge (approx: 300 tons with machinery) whole, and deposit on the quay for subsequent dismantling and sale. If this is not possible to accomplish the swing bridge will be dismantled by mobile crane on the Sharpness abutments, loading the sections on to rail wagons or canal barges.

11. Lift off span 18–19, 163 tons.

12. After span 18–19 is removed thereby clearing pier 19 (group of four columns) slings and chains will be attached to span 19–20 for subsequent lifting. Pier 19 four columns complete will be winched over, breaking off piers, allowing the span to fall into the river. Utilising the slings and chains previously attached the crane will lift one end of the span until a section is above water, this will then be cut off, repeating until the whole span is deposited on shore.

13. Repeat on span 20–21.

14. Lift off span 21.

15. Winch over pier 21 complete and deposit on west shore.

16. Commence breaking up piers, their removal will be achieved by one of two methods,
    (a) snapping by "winching over" or
    (b) if piers are anchored to the rock foundations, apply a direct lift
         of 600 tons to attempt to raise piers straight out of the foundations.

130

Phase Two

The viaduct on the west bank will be utilised for transporting scrap metal from the site and a 10 ton crane will be positioned over masonry pillar 1 to convey metal from the shore to lorries or rail wagons on the viaduct. A passenger hoist will be provided for quick access to the shore.

1. On completion of the cutting operations, the viaduct will be drilled and prepared for explosives. At a time suitable to British Railways and when the South Wales line has been protected, the complete viaduct will be demolished. The charges will be placed and exploded by Woodcroft Construction Company Limited (British Railways contractor for the demolition of Dowdeswell Viaduct near Cheltenham). The debris on the line will be removed by loading shovel.

2. Simultaneously with 1, the swing bridge pier will be demolished by hand and debris spread on the shore.

3. Sharpness abutments dismantled by grab crane and deposited in the cutting.

4. Rails and sleepers will be taken up when no longer required.

Preliminary work at the bridge site, fencing off Severn Bridge Station, removing rails and sleepers, commenced on 28 July. *Magnus II* was due to leave Hamburg on 14 August and Nordman Construction Company's demolition team would be moving in on Monday 21 August.

Magnus II arrives

Ulrich Harms floating crane *Magnus II* arrived at Sharpness on 22 August at 9.30a.m. piloted up river by D. Griffey of the Severn Pilots, and the remainder of the day was spent erecting its flying jib.

Magnus II was an excellent example of modern crane engineering, though towed by tug from Hamburg, the crane possessed its own diesel electric propulsion system with four steering screws at each corner of the hull and was capable of pivoting about its own centre line. To counterbalance the added weight on the jib when lifting, water could be pumped into ballast tanks at the stern, thus maintaining the vessel at even keel. The total lifting capacity being 400 tons to a height of 150 feet rendered it fully capable of lifting all the bridge spans except the two 312 foot spans over the navigation channel, which weighed approximately 530 tons.

With the cost of hire to the Nordman Construction Company being

1,000 guineas per day, it was obvious that, with these costs in mind, *Magnus II* should be operating with the utmost economy, taking advantage of two tides as stated in Phase One, paragraph nine of Nordman's schedule, but as is typical of the day, even the best laid plans are apt to go astray, and the series of events which followed were to produce disastrous results for Nordmans.

DIARY OF OPERATIONS BY MAGNUS II

23 August

Magnus II leaves Sharpness at 10.00 hours, proceeding to bridge site. Remainder of the day spent practising manoeuvres at fixing moorings.

24 August

174 foot span between piers 18 – 19 off at 08.00–09.30 hours with the crane working on upstream side of the bridge. 174 foot span between piers 15 – 16 lifted at 16.00 hours, advantage of two tides.

25 August

Military trestling lifted at 10.30, F.R.L. Barnwell, C.C.E. visited the site and crane.

26 August

174 foot span between piers 14 – 15 lifted 10.30 hours.

27 August

134 foot span between pier 21 and viaduct lifted 11.30 hours. C.C.E. again at the site.

28 August

Work commenced on group of four piers 19, one column supporting 312 foot span bombarded with crane hook to produce a large breach, a hawser round the group of piers used to collapse the pier when the strain was taken by the crane. Lift attempted at 15.30 hours but unsuccessful. Cross bracings bombarded with crane hook.

29 August

Yesterday's operations suspended and 134 foot span between piers 13 – 14 lifted at 13.00 hours. Demolition ball brought to the site for renewed attempt on pier 19.

30 August

Pier bombarded with ball, producing larger breach, strain taken at 14.55 hours, pier collapsed, span falling to river bed.

31 August

Span reported in three pieces below low water level. Crane removing parts of span.

1 September

Crane bombards pier 20 with ball, span between piers 20 – 21 falls at 15.45 hours.

2 and 3 September

Two days spent recovering broken spans from river bed.

4 September

134 foot spans between piers 12 – 13 and 11 – 12 lifted.

5 September

Gale force winds; operations suspended for the day.

6 September

134 foot span between piers 10 – 11 lifted and deposited near the swing bridge.

7 September

134 foot spans 9 – 10 and 8 – 9 lifted.

8 September

134 foot span 7 – 8 lifted.

9 September

134 foot span 6 – 7 lifted.

10 September

134 foot spans 5 – 6 and 4 – 5 lifted.

11 September

Magnus II prepares to leave for Hamburg.

With the departure of *Magnus II* imminent, an on site meeting had been held at Sharpness on Wednesday 30 August, attended by the district civil engineer, J. Tyrer, H. Morgan Nordman Construction Company, British Waterways and the Severn River Authority. British Waterways expressed their concern regarding the removal of the swing bridge by the floating crane and suggested successive balanced oxy-acetylene cutting of the girder work, a safer method, should any accident occur in lifting, with the resulting damage to the canal bank.

The Severn River Authority granted permission for ten spans to be deposited on the foreshore adjacent to pier 1, for final cutting and removal via the swing bridge.

The meeting finally concluded by leaving Nordman Construction Company to devise a suitable scheme to meet their requirements.

Magnus II was now gone, leaving behind an account for the sum of £21,000, twenty-one piers, three spans and the swing bridge still remaining, awaiting removal. It was obvious all was not well, the crane had not been operated round the clock as previously stated, the method of removing the piers by "winching over" to snap them off or lifting bodily from the foundations, was extremely dubious, in view of the size of the piers and also in view of the thousands of tons of "pitching" deposited around the foundations during the life of the bridge. It was also doubtful if *Magnus* could be operated close in shore on the east bank to lift the swing bridge complete, bearing in mind that the jib must be in a near vertical position to provide the optimum lifting conditions.

On 19 September, Nordman Construction Company produced a new schedule as follows:

1. Crane moving onto viaduct 20 September 1967.

2. Bulk Oxygen tank installed with feed lines to the viaduct base.

3. Commence cutting and loading bridge sections and transport from site.

4. Dismantle military trestle.

River

1. Arrange for diver to inspect navigation channel.

2. All pier sections to be removed by floating grab.

3. Demolish all pier stumps to "pitching" level by explosives. Drilling will blast at high water.

4. Remaining legs of trestle to be sheared by explosives.

Sharpness

1. Rails and sleepers on swing bridge to Sharpness station removed,
    balast levelled and road prepared.

2. Position crane on swing bridge, cut spans and remove.

Lift-off for the first 134 foot span at Purton

D. Knight

Derelict Severn Bridge Station with Magnus II woorking in the background.

R. Huxley

3.   Clear foreshore, remaining piers to be dropped by explosives. Cast iron sections to be broken up and transported, concrete left to disperse.

4.   Cut up spans on foreshore and transport. Remaining piers blasted.

Swing bridge

Programme prepared and consult British Waterways. Scrap to be loaded into barges. Masonry to be removed as previous schedule. Underwater survey to be carried out in conjunction with interested authorities.

Weather

We had anticipated starting the contract early in the spring, but dismantling did not commence until 24 August. It would be advantageous to complete demolition by November but the weather and tides will prove an important factor.

All efforts will be made regarding continuity of the work.

An echo sounding survey was carried out to determine the effects of debris left in the navigation channel and to facilitate its subsequent removal. The survey took place on 25 September with sweeps up and downstream of the pillars in the navigation channel.

The messy work of cutting up the spans on the west bank was now proceeding, a rather irksome task, that was not assisted by tidal and weather conditions, and being further prolonged by having to cut throught the bridge trusses several times, due to the original design in using laminations to make up the required thickness of the trusses.

Demolition of the viaduct

In the meantime, plans were being formulated for the demolition of the masonry viaduct, adjacent to Severn Bridge Station.

It was essential to demolish the viaduct, prior to using any explosives on the river piers, when the resultant shock waves could possibly bring the viaduct down on the South Wales line.

At a site meeting at Severn Bridge Station on 6 November, it was suggested that Nordman Construction Company should arrange the programme for demolition, stressing the fact the any delay after 31 December would interfere with a programmed blockade of the Severn Tunnel, which should continue until Easter (1968). If possible, opera-

Entitled 'The End of an Era' this photograph appeared in the National Press; it shows the dropping of the first 312 foot span, disintegrating as it falls it presented a number of problems when attempting to salvage the wreckage.

The Press Association

Magnus II at work retrieving span No. 20 from the river bed.

D. Knight

tions should be speeded up and completed by Christmas with regard to the removal of scrap metal across the viaduct.

Nordman Construction Company had already invited an explosives expert to inspect the viaduct and carry out a test of explosives on the wrought iron work. The tests were concluded on 21 November and a further date was arranged for the inspection of the viaduct.

H. Morgan and the explosives expert completed the inspection of the viaduct on 11 December. The expert was satisfied that 'there appeared to be no reason against using the standard procedure, as indicated on their pamphlet on demolition. Three rows of holes dipping at forty-five degrees drilled in both sides of the pillars adjacent to the South Wales line. He suggested a fourth row of holes should be added on the faces remote from the railway, dipping at forty-five degrees finishing just short of the centre line. It was hoped that by breaking the pillars higher on one side, that they would be induced to fall away from the railway. Double rows of holes would be required at the key and springing points of the arches. There appeared to be no reason why the contractor should not demolish the viaduct at one blast. Cordtex detonating fuses should be used to initiate the charges, with a system of closed rings with double lines used for all the trunk lines.'

In view of the large amount of drilling to be done, it was now obvious that the viaduct would not be demolished on or before 31 December, the news of which, brought Nordman Construction Company a sharp reply from the district civil engineer, demanding an explanation for the delay in view of the emphasis on the necessity of completing the job by 31 December.

The viaduct is blown

Negotiations were now proceeding on the question of who should blow the viaduct. Nordman Construction Company wanted Underwater Welders Limited of Cardiff while British Railways favoured Swinnerton & Miller Limited of Willenhall. Eventually it was decided that Swinnerton & Miller should be engaged.

The date fixed for the blowing of the viaduct was Sunday 10 March 1968 and the notes of a site meeting on 5 February provides the schedule of the days events as follows:

(a) Precautions prior to demolition.

Hand signalmen to be stationed below the viaduct during the clearing of the parapets and 'fill' on the span over the railway, which will be carried out under a 'between trains' occupation by local arrangement. A

Two photographs show the problems encountered in salvaging the two 312' spans; the disintegration of the spans as they fell and silting left a large amount of metal unclaimed on the river bed.

J. Ashford

telephone to be provided on the box to box circuit.

When the contractor starts loading the bore holes with explosives, a hand signalman to be provided on each side of the viaduct at a distance of approximately one mile, viz., at Permanent Way Cabins at 129m, 50c and 131m 63c. A hand signalman is required on a twenty-four hour basis until the viaduct is blown. The contractor will provide a watchman to guard the explosive stores. It is anticipated that it will take two or three days to place all the charges.

(b) Occupations, Sunday 10 March 1968.

Up line, 05.00–16,00 hours – Absolute – following the passage of the 01.20 Paddington.

Down line 01.30–20.00 hours – Absolute – in conjunction with relaying.

T.R.S.'s

Down line 20 miles per hour from 130m 57c to 131m 15c in conjunction with relaying as above, and

Up line 20 miles per hour from 130m 67c continuing until further notice.

Sunday 10 March 1968

03.00 hours – Remove down line on either side of viaduct.

05.00 hours – Remove up line on either side of viaduct.

for a maximum of 3 lengths on either side of viaduct, in each case.

07.00 hours approximately Contractor to blow viaduct and remove debris from railway line and prepare formation to receive track.

13.00 hours – Relay up line and fettle for 20 miles per hour.

16.00 hours – Re-open up line for traffic to be followed as soon as possible by the down line

On 8 March Swinnerton & Miller's team commenced loading the bore holes, completing the operation on 10 March. The whole operation had been treated as a top secret exercise and at dawn on Sunday 10 March, only a handful of spectators, other than railway workers were present to witness the blowing of Griffith Griffith's viaduct. The Severn was in one of its more passive moods, with hardly a ripple on its surface. The roar of bulldozers could be heard beneath the viaduct, pushing away tons of ballast for re-use later in the day, the scene being lit by the glare of floodlights.

As seven o'clock was approaching and word went round that the blast had been postponed for twenty minutes. At approximately

The stark scene from the Sharpness end of the bridge as Magnus II works in the background; note the spans deposited on the shore at Purton ready for cutting up.

R. Huxley

Russell Adams, FRPS, who earned world wide fame for air to air photography at the Gloster Aircraft Company, was commissioned by the River Severn Authority to carry out an aerial survey in the vicinity of the bridge

Russell Adams FRPS,
by courtesy of Mr. L. Haines, Engineer, Severn River Authority

Griffith Griffiths viaduct dropped by high explosives in March 1968.

R. Lane

As the smoke clears half of the viaduct remains standing. Henry Morgan remarked later 'This is a stubborn old bridge'.

R. Lane

7.30a.m. the roar of the bulldozers ceased, and the workmen could be seen silhouetted against the dawn sky, climbing the steep embankment to the safety of the Severn Bridge Station. A further postponement of the blast was announced and a deathly silence fell on the scene, broken only by the squealing of gulls and distant voices. The silence was broken by three blasts on a Klaxon horn on the embankment, followed a minute later by another blast, at 7.40a.m. clouds of smoke appeared along the viaduct, followed seconds later by the roar of high explosives and falling masonry echoing across the river and back, and as the smoke cleared, it was seen that six arches on the eastern side of the South Wales line were still standing. A further examination showed them badly shattered at their bases and now standing in an extremely precarious condition. Henry Morgan remarked later, 'This is a stubborn old bridge.'

The work of clearing the South Wales line was long and difficult, bearing in mind that many of the stones weighed two tons or more, but the line was eventually restored for traffic at 10.00p.m.

During the week the six standing arches were re-drilled and plans were made to complete the demolition on Friday 15 March, on a 'between trains occupation' basis. On this occasion the work was carried out by L. Devenish of Wells, but again the bridge was stubborn to the end, one pillar remained standing and it was later toppled over by winching.

Demolition had now been proceeding for eight months, the slick, swift operation promised by Nordman Construction Company had not materialised, neither had the sixty skilled steel erectors, only a mere half a dozen or so men had contributed to the operations. A certain amount of extra work had been introduced into the contract which included the removal of the track from Severn Bridge Station to Lydney, but this did not present any great problem, but at this stage, the end of the project was not in sight.

Instructions from British Railways on 25 March requested that the contractor should proceed urgently with the following items:— 'Tidy the debris at the viaduct, clear piers and masonry on the shore, dismantle trestling, remove all obstructions from the channel, remove thirteen piers from the river, dismantle six remaining in the river, remove swing bridge and pier and Sharpness abutments.'

The contractor in difficulties

In April Nordman Construction Company were seeking an interim payment of £30,000 in respect of the contract, but no provision existed in the terms of the contract for such a payment, the tender having clearly stated that payment would be made at the satisfactory conclusion of the contract. Nordman Construction Company claimed that extra costs had been incurred in removing obstructions and that extended credit facilities were now not readily available at the banks, but British Railways were adamant that they were under no obligation to concede an interim payment.

Nordman Construction Company proceeded with the clearing of the underwater obstructions and in June reported that the channel was clear to twenty foot below datum. In the meantime, it was learned that a writ had been filed in the High Court. Ulrich Harms versus The Nordman Construction Company Limited and a counterclaim and defence filed by Nordman Construction Company. It appeared that payment had been withheld from the Germans when Ulrich Harms claimed the crane had been hired on the terms of '1,000 guineas per day' while Nordman Construction Company claimed it had been hired at 1,000 guineas per twenty-four hours.

Under the terms of contract between contractor and sub-contractor, this was of no concern to British Railways, being purely a question of interpretation of the terms 'day' as opposed to twenty-four hours. It was further learned that payments had been withheld from Swinnerton & Miller in respect of the viaduct demolition, Nordman Construction Company claiming they did not consider Swinnerton & Miller as sub-contractors, claiming they were 'forced on them'.

Eventually, British Railways conceded to Nordman Construction Company's requests and quoted an interim payment in respect of the contract.

Demolition proceeded with the cutting of spans on the east bank and Nordman Construction Company had now purchased the *Severn King* previously owned by the Old Passage Ferry, which had ceased to operate, with the opening of the Severn road bridge. A mobile crane had been installed on the *Severn King's* turn-table and scrap metal was being transported via Sharpness Docks.

Prior to obtaining the demolition contract, Nordman Construction Company had been mainly a road construction firm and at this state in the proceedings, a new line of thought occurred. The idea was to use the remaining undemolished portion of the bridge (three spans and the swing bridge) as a jetty. Nordman Construction Company, at this time, possessed a tarmac processing plant at their Gloucester establishment, stone being shipped from quarries near the River Wye, via the Severn and Berkeley Canal to Gloucester for processing. The plan was to breach the vessels at the end of the remaining portion of the bridge, grab off the stone by crane into lorries and transport via Sharpness station to Gloucester, therefore making a considerable saving in canal fees. The idea was an admirable one for a company now beginning to face financial difficulties, but British Railways would not agree, reminding Nordman Construction Company of the terms of the contract and the objections which would follow from British Waterways and the County planning officer.

On Wednesday 20 November, it was learned that Mr. D.V. Mundy had been appointed receiver and general manager for Nordman Construction Company.

In a statement to the press, Henry Morgan said that the six year old Company, with a turnover of £500,000 per annum, had paid off eighty employees and work had ceased on six other contracts worth £400,000, but if the receiver allowed work on the bridge contract to be completed, the Company could finish with a surplus. Morgan blamed the credit squeeze and the existing government for their present state of affairs.

Nordmans had by this time been paid £50,000 in respect of the Severn Bridge contract, but the expense incurred in removing obstructions and loss of metal, had been borne by the Company's insurance. The high cost of the hire of *Magnuss II* had no doubt contributed to the Company's predicament, for had the crane been working 'round the clock' as previously forecast, its presence would have been needed for approximately nine days. The resale of the bridge spans did not materialise, although it was hoped to sell the swing bridge to the U.S.A. where it could be re-erected as an example of Victorian engineering.

British Railways were now faced with two prospects:

(a) a new contract for the remaining demolition work or

(b) to complete the work themselves.

A plan had now been formulated which included action to be taken should the receiver decide to withdraw from the contract which is outlined below:

(a) Appoint a full time supervisor.

(b) Negotiate terms for formally taking over the *Severn King* and equipment.

(c) Arrange separate contract for the demolition of the swing bridge.

(d) Swinnerton & Miller Limited to carry out the blasting of remaining piers.

(e) Investigate the possibility of taking over Nordman Construction Company's labour on similar terms, self employed, labour only, sub-contractors.

It was eventually decided by the receiver that Nordman Construction Company would go into liquidation and the Company would therefore take no further part in the demolition. At the same time British Railways was approached by the father of H. Morgan, Mr. W. Morgan, with a view to taking over the remaining work, confessing that he had no business interests in the Nordman Construction Company. British Railways decided to proceed with their present plans and V. Harris of the district civil engineer's department, was appointed demolition supervisor. An inspection of the pier stumps remaining in the channel was carried out on Friday 6 December with W. Hardy of Newnham-on-Severn providing the boat for the occasion. W. Hardy had been employed by Nordman Construction Company as river adviser while *Magnus II* was operating at the site and his knowledge of tidal conditions had been sought on numerous other occasions by British Railways.

The Severn King wrecked

The remaining three spans at the east bank were dropped by explosive charges during January 1969, a crane on the swing bridge removed the scrap and the *Severn King* removed the metal which was out of reach of the crane.

Swinnerton & Miller were once again employed in demolishing the pier stumps remaining in the navigation channel, the stumps being drilled twelve feet deep with five holes in each cylinder. The charges were connected to a three hundred foot long firing cable and fired by hand on board the *Severn King* at high water. In some cases, charges were fired from the Waveridge sands.

The *Severn King*, registered at Newport, a steel hull, twin screw, car ferry boat weighing eighty-three tons gross, was built at Beverley, Yorks in 1935 for the Old Passage Ferry Company Limited, and had been extensively employed during the final stages of river work, but on the evening tide of Friday 4 July the *King* broke adrift and became impaled on the stump of pier no. 2.

The tide that evening was 27.4 feet. Prior to high water, the bow mooring rope parted, allowing the *King* to swing on the stern mooring and drift onto the pier stump, at ebb tide the vessel settled down with a list to starboard of forty-five degrees. V. Harris, the demolition supervisor arrived at the site at 07.45 next day and an inspection of the vessel revealed a hole amidships two foot long by six inches wide, approximately two foot up from the keel. With a period of neap tides imminent, salvage work was out of the question, but the high tides forecast for the end of the month would produce ideal conditions for refloating the *King*.

On Sunday 27 July the first state of the refloating operation commenced with a concrete box being placed over the hole in the vessel's hull, the materials being transported from Sharpness by boat. W. Hardy was once again enlisted to assist and advise in a long, tedious round the clock operation which ended on the evening of 29 July. During this

146

Messrs. Swinnerton and Miller drop three remaining spans near the Gloucester and Berkeley Canal.

R. Huxley

Pier stumps being drilled prior to blasting. A portable crane and air compressors were installed on the deck of the 'Severn King'.

Vic Harris

147

period, continuous heavy rain made working conditions almost un-
bearable.

Two Uniflote pontoons were towed to the site from Sharpness and
fixed to the sides of the *Severn King* and all bulk head doors sealed.
Timber shoring was erected under the vessel's bow to ensure that if
floated off the stump in the correct direction. Failure to do so would
have resulted in enlarging the hole in the vessel's hull. Finally a winch
was installed on the shore linked to the vessel by a 200 foot nylon rope.

The *King* was refloated on the evening tide of July 28, a further
twenty-four hours spent winching the vessel in shore, where it was
made ready to proceed to Sharpness, an operation that was concluded
on the evening tide of July 29.

After thirty years of ferry service, brought to an abrupt end by the
opening of the Severn Road Bridge, the *Severn King's* final voyage
ended in being beached near the entrance to Sharpness Docks. The
engines were salvaged and at the time of writing the hull is partially cut
up; once again the River Severn had taken its toll.

During September the remaining piers across the Ridge were drilled
and demolished. The method used on that occasion was by fixing a
long rope from the farthest pier to the bank, to which the firing cable
was attached by tape. A number of fishing net floats were then threaded
along the rope and firing cable to allow the whole assembly to float on
the incoming tide; mooring the rope at both ends ensured that the firing
cable was not washed away. The charges were fired by hand on the east
bank adjacent to the swing bridge.

Sharpness swing bridge disappears

The final phase of demolition, was the removal of Sharpness swing
bridge under a separate contract by Underwater Welders Limited, of
Cardiff, a contract which also called for the demolition of pier one, a
masonry column of considerable size and double the bridge width.

Stage one consisted in removing the signal box and engine house,
engines and boilers; following this, the span was successively cut at
each end. A motorised winch was installed on the two arch viaduct, for
lowering portions of the span to the tow path, there to be reduced to a
more manageable size.

Compared with the previous stages of demolition, the removal of te
swing bridge was an extremely slick operation, taking only a few
weeks.

On Sunday 25 January 1970, the last remaining portions of the bridge
structure disappeared.

Pier stumps being blown at high tide; the explosive charges were fired from the deck of the Severn King

Vic Harris

The swing bridge partially demolished by Underwater Welders Ltd., of Roath Basin, Cardiff.

R. Huxley

The swing bridge masonry pier and two arch viaduct stands as a last monument to the first and only major railway bridge to span the River Severn.

R. Huxley

The end of demolition was the dropping of pier one by high explosives. Drilling of the pier commenced in March and on 13 May, the curtain came down on the final act of the demolition of the Severn Bridge.

Like the other railways of the Forest of Dean, the Severn & Wye and Severn Bridge Railway is now virtually extinct; all that remains are two sections, Berkeley Road – Sharpness and Lydney Junction – Parkend. The track beyond Sharpness to the Severn Bridge has been removed and the North Docks Branch has also been severed from the main line. Sharpness station with its well kept flower beds surrounded by white-washed stone, presents a desolate scene nowadays and is nothing more than two platforms separated by a gulf of weeds.

Severn Bridge Station, with its expansive view of the 'Severn Sea'[3] and the Cotswolds, has suffered a similar fate, and nearby, the vast mound of masonry of Griffith Griffith's viaduct, is slowly sinking into the bank of the river. However, across the Severn, Sharpness Docks still enjoys a considerable amount of prosperity and, unlike other docks, is unsullied by the present day labour problems. In the winter months, vast cargoes of timber from Russian ports can be seen arriving at regular intervals, and the dock still provides the gateway to the Port of

150

Gloucester, and at the time of writing, is udergoing considerable expansion and modernisation.

Lydney Docks, however, has not enjoyed the prosperity of Sharpness, small cargoes of logs for the Pine End Works are the only imports of this once bustling port. But a metamorphosis has taken place, one which was never envisaged by its original proprietors, the berths and banks once occupied by the Severn trows and that scruffy little collier the *Black Dwarf* have taken on a new and more picturesque look, provided by the weekend sailor with trim pleasure craft of infinite variety dotting the banks.

The Harbour Master's residence, built by the Severn & Wye and Severn Bridge Railway Company in 1894, is now the headquarters of the local yacht cl;ub and the estuary once feared by the more professional sailors, provides endless amusements for the weekenders.

Keeling's two great masterpieces, the Severn Bridge and Lydbrook viaduct are now gone and with them has died a type of civil engineering that we shall never see employed again.

Many sidelong glances are being cast at our modern bridges, of the box girder type with their suspect methods of erection which has taken an alarming toll of human lives, but there is no doubt that when the present problems are solved, they will last equally as long as Keeling's structures.

References to Chapter Seven

1. *The Gloucester Journal* 11 February 1939.
2. *The Citizen* 7 March 1967.
3. The Gloucester and Sharpness Steam Packet Company's: *Handbook and Timetable* describing the view of the river at Sharpness. The handbook advertised "Delightful water cruises to Gloucester".

This Chapter is based on information from the district civil engineer's files, British Rail, Western Region, Gloucester.

CHAPTER EIGHT

General Engineering and Operational Data (Severn & Wye Joint Railway)

This chapter is intended to provide the reader with information regarding the operation of the Severn & Wye Joint Railway, and is based on extracts from "The Appendix to Service Time Tables 1932, L.M.S. and G.W.R., Severn & Wye Joint Line".

As this publication deals mainly with the Severn Bridge it is intended that the extracts will only cover that portion of the railway in the immediate vicinity of the bridge, namely Lydney Town to Berkeley Road.

Some engineering data and explanation of technical terms are also included in respect of the Severn Bridge.

Block systems Lydney Town – Berkeley Road

The London Midland and Scottish Standard Regulations for signalling by Absolute Block Telegraph on double lines of railway were in force over the undermentioned double line block sections:–

> Sharpness South Box and Sharpness Station Box.
> Lydney Junction (Otters Pool Box) and Lydney Engine Shed Box.
> Lydney Engine Shed Box and Lydney Town Box

The London Midland and Scottish Standard Block Regulations for single lines worked on the Electric Train Tablet or Electric Train Token or Electric Train Staff Block System were in force over the undermentioned block sections:–

> Berkeley Road Station and Berkeley Loop Junction.
> Berkeley Loop Junction and Sharpness South Box.
> Sharpness Station Box and Severn Bridge Station Box.
> Severn Bridge Station and Lydney Junction (Otters Pool Box). The Great Western Standard Block Regulations for double lines were in force between Otters Pool Box (Lydney Junction, Severn & Wye) and Lydney East Box, Great Western Railway.

The London Midland & Scottish Standard Regulations for signalling by Absolute Block Telegraph on double lines of railway were in force

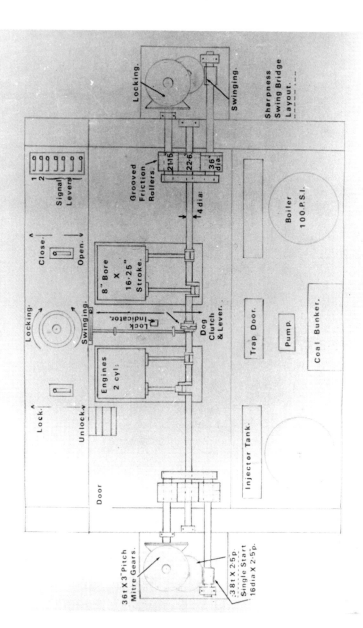

Sharpness Swing Bridge signal box showing the layout of the engines, boilers and driving gear.

Chief Mechanical Engineer, British Rail, Swindon

between Berkeley Loop Junction and Berkeley Road South Junction (L.M.S.).

Up and down lines

Trains running in the direction of Berkeley Road from Lydney Town were designated 'Up Trains' and those from Berkeley Road to Lydney Town were designated 'Down Trains'.

The working of trains over the Severn Bridge

Trains running over the Severn Bridge must not be worked by more than one engine in front. Two engines coupled together must not, under any circumstances, be run over the bridge.

In the event of the failure of an engine at either end of the bridge and its being necessary for such engine to be taken to the opposite end, or if an engine fails on the bridge, arrangements must be made for the engine to be worked specially and four wagons must be placed between the assisting engine and the disabled engine. A competent man must in all cases ride upon the disabled engine.

The following are the only engines that were allowed to pass over the Severn Bridge.

GREAT WESTERN ENGINES

0–6–0 class Nos. 363, 2301 to 2360, 2381 to 2490, 2511 to 2580
0–6–0 (tank) 2021 to 2160

L.M.S. FREIGHT ENGINES

No. 1 class bearing numbers between 2399 and 2867
No. 2 class bearing numbers between 2900 and 3129

NOTE engines of other classes bearing numbers as above must not be allowed to pass over the Bridge.

L.M.S. PASSENGER ENGINES

No. 1 class (Precedent Type 2–4–0 straight link – Nos. 5000, 5001, 5005, 5011, 5014, 5018, 5021, 5027, 5050, 5069, 5070
No. 1 class (Waterloo) type 2–4–0 straight link – No. 5095

The point to point times for trains were, Lydney to Berkeley Loop Junction, passenger trains eighteen minutes, freight trains, thirty minutes, the distance being six miles, seventy-three chains.

The Severn Bridge was restricted with a speed of fifteen miles per hour, or three minutes for the crossing, as displayed on the notice boards at each end of the bridge.

Engine whistles

Standard Whistle Code – Applicable unless otherwise shown herein.

Main Line	1 whistle
Relief Line	2 whistles
To or from platform loops	2 whistles
Branch lines	3 whistles
Goods lines	4 whistles
To engine sheds	2 short whistles
Yards, to or from	4 short whistles
Crossover road	Main line – 1 crow and 1 whistle.
	Relief line – 1 crow and 2 whistles
In siding clear of running lines	3 short whistles

Special station and junction whistles

Lydney Docks over G.W. Line:–

East to Dock Sidings	3
East to West side	2 and 1 crow
Dock Sidings to West side	1 crow
Dock Sidings to East side	1 long 1 short
West to Docks	2
Docks to West	2 short and 1 long

Drivers must sound their whistles when approaching the undermentioned crossings:–

Oldminster Level Crossing (Station side of Sharpness South Box).

Sharpness swing bridge locking devices

(a) Tapper-bell communications between the Severn Bridge Station Box and Swing Bridge Box and between the Swing Bridge Box and Sharpness Station Box.

(b) Electric locks on the up starting signal lever in the Severn Bridge Station Box; on the down starting signal lever bolting the Bridge in the

155

Swing Bridge Box and means of releasing then in case of failure.

(c)   A special tapper-key in the Severn Bridge Station Box for releasing the lock on the Sharpness Station Box down starting signal lever, and a special tapper-key in the Sharpness Station Box for releasing the lock on the Severn Bridge Station up starting signal lever.

These special tapper-keys were also used for releasing the lock on the lever bolting the Bridge.

(d)   Lock indicators in connection with each of the Three Electric Locks showing whether the locks were 'On', 'Off' or 'Wrong'.

(e)   An electric switch worked by lever No. 1 in the Swing Bridge Box which, when the lever was in its normal position, prevented a tablet being withdrawn or the locks taken off the starting signals at each end of the Tablet Section.

(f)   An electric indicator to show whether the Swing Bridge Pawl had fallen into proper position. This indicator shows "Pawl In" on a white disc and "Pawl Out" on a red disc.

(g)   Telephonic communication between Severn Bridge Station Box, Swing Bridge Box and Sharpness Station Box.

(h)   A bolting lever, No. 2 in the Swing Bridge Box for bolting the Bridge.

(i)   Single needle through circuit, each of the Boxes being connected with it.

(j)   A mechanical indicator in the Swing Bridge Box, to show when the Swing Bridge is in position for bolting with lever No. 2.

The working of trains over the Severn Bridge

Special electrical locking appliances and Block instruments were installed to prevent a tablet being withdrawn at Severn Bridge Station or Sharpness Station Box at a time when the swing bridge was not in a position to receive trains or engines. The system also ensured that the swing bridge would not operate once a driver had received the tablet to enter the section and the starting signals had been lowered.

The system, however, did not dispense wih use of fixed hand, or detonating signals when such signals were requisite to protect obstructions on the line, neither did they dispense with the regulations for train signalling on the E.T.T. Block system.

The normal position for the swing bridge, while the railway was open for traffic, was for the railway, but free to be swung or opened for the passage of canal traffic. Should a failure in the bell system occur between the signal boxes involved, the names of the bell signals were

Bell Signals Between Severn Bridge Station Box and Swing Bridge Box
and Between Swing Bridge Box and Sharpness Station Box

See Clause		Beats on Bell	How to be Given
1	Call attention	1	
3	* Is line clear for passenger train?	4	3 pause 1
3	* Is line clear for goods, mineral or ballast train?	3	3 consecutively
3	* Is line clear for light engine or engine and brake?	5	2 pause 3
3	Line clear	3	1 pause 2
3	* Train arrived, ready to unlock bridge	3	2 pause 1
3	* Train arrived, but another train	5	3 pause 2
3	waiting	6	6 consecutively
4	Obstruction danger	8	3 pause 5
3	Cancelling 'is line clear' signal	2	2 consecutively
3	Release Bridge Lock	4	2 pause 2
11	Bridge unlocked	16	16 consecutively
11	* Testing bells	16	4 pause 4 pause 4 pause 4
8	* Lock Bridge for testing	15	5 pause 5 pause 5
9	* Opening of signal box	17	7 pause 5 pause 5
9	* Closing of signal box	16	8 pause 8
12	* Testing complete	20	5 pause 5 pause 5 pause 5
	* Testing controlled or slotted signals		

Note: These signals are to be given on the tapper bells.

Bell or Gong Signals Between Severn Bridge Station Box and Sharpness Station Box

See Clause		Beats on Bell	How to be Given
3	Release starting signal	7	3 pause 4
3	Starting signal lowered	7	4 pause 3

Note: These signals are to be given on the train tablet instruments passed over the telephone, and if the telephone had also failed, the single needle speaking circuit was employed and signals were recorded in the usual way.

Releasing arrangements were provided at the Swing Bridge Signal Box to enable No. 2 lever, which bolts bridge, to be released when it was necessary for the section to be worked by a pilot man.

Releasing apparatus was also provided in connection with the electric locks on the starting signal levers in the Severn Bridge Station and Sharpness Station signal boxes to enable the starting signals to be released in the case of failure of the electrical apparatus. In the event of a signalman, after obtaining a tablet, being unable to move his starting signal lever when the signalman at the opposite end of the section holds down his special tapper-key to release it, he must break the glass front of the box, press the stud within the box and while the stud is being pressed lower the starting signal. The signalman must immediately report the circumstance to the Station Master or person in charge of the station and the lineman at Gloucester (London Midland and Scottish) must be advised in accordance with the instructions. When the apparatus has been repaired the lineman must renew the glass front and seal the box.

The fact that the glass had been broken must be reported in the train register book and the circumstances reported to the Chief General Superintendent, Derby.

The operation of the swing bridge for canal traffic

A signal was located on the swing bridge for the purpose of indicating to vessels on the canal whether the bridge could or could not be opened.

The signal arm was extended horizontally when the bridge could not be opened and a red light was displayed at night, it was lowered in the normal manner showing a green light when it was safe for vessels to proceed. A white light at each end of the swing bridge denoted that it was open parallel with the canal.

Vessels were required to give three whistles, if capable of doing so, at least four hundred yards from the bridge and move slowly up to the bridge and be prepared to stop one hundred yards distant, the bridge signalman answering with three whistles when the bridge was fully open. He was required to be on the alert for vessels which were unable to give the prescribed whistles.

These regulations applied only to vessels with masts higher than the base of the swing bridge structure.

Safety systems during the maintenance of the swing bridge

Three keys were provided in connection with the lock on the clutch gear wheel to be used on the signalman's authority by the bridge maintenance foreman, ganger, linesman or cleaner in charge of repairs or painting. This enabled the workmen engaged to carry out their work and to prevent the bridge being rotated while the workmen were in such a position as to sustain injury.

The keys were lettered 'Severn Bridge' and were so interlocked that none of them could be removed from the lock on the clutch gear wheel unless the wheel and bridge bolt lever No. 2 are in the normal position. The clutch gear wheel could only be turned to enable the bridge to be moved or the wedges being operated and No. 2 lever could only be pulled when the keys were in position.

In all cases the removal of the keys was reported to the Station Master at Sharpness and the Engineer's bridge inspector. An endless chain apparatus was provided to lower the keys to the person in charge of maintenance who removed the keys on the chain which was immediately reported to the persons previously mentioned.

Should a train or vessel require to pass while the work was in progress the signalman gave three beats on a gong fixed outside the box, the person in charge was required, as quickly as possible, to ensure that everything was safe and transfer the keys back to the box.

The loss of a key, or keys, was covered by three duplicate sets installed in the swing bridge box, in glass fronted boxes. Upon the loss of a key the person to whom it had been delivered must satisfy himself that it could not be recovered in time and proceed to the box and enter in the train record book 'Bridge Key lost, bridge may be moved', signing his name. The signalman may then break the glass and extract a new key, he then immediately advised the Traffic Inspector, the London Midland and Scottish District Signal and Telegraph Assistant, Birmingham and the Engineer's Bridge Inspector by telegraph, that a key had been lost, the duplicate key being used until the original was recovered.

Swing bridge staff duties

The engine driver must be competent to work the electrical instruments, signals, locking apparatus etc., and must do so when a signalman is not on duty. The signalman or signalmen must be competent to work the engines, turn the Bridge and attend to the fires, and must do so when the engine driver is not on duty.

The engine driver must keep the engines and all the machinery clean and in good order, and the signalmen must assist the engine driver in

Inside the Swing Bridge Signal Box showing both engines, one in use, one in reserve.
Chief Mechanical Engineer, British Rail, Swindon

coaling and cleaning the engines.

When the railway was closed during a portion of the night, the man on the early turn must be on duty in time to have the engines in steam ready for turning the Bridge at least twenty minutes before the first train was due to pass Sharpness Station or Severn Bridge Station as the case may be, and the man on the late turn must bank the fires after the last train has passed and the Bridge has been opened.

The engine driver must carefully attend to the following directions for keeping the engines, boilers and machinery in good order:–

The boilers to be worked separately and changed every fortnight. Each boiler, after having worked a fortnight to be thoroughly washed out, and the firebars taken out, the tubes and firebox cleaned out. The safety valves should be tested daily by easing the valves.

The lead plugs in firebox to be taken out, examined and, if necessary, changed and safety valves, connections, pressure gauges, blow-off cock and other fittings examined, cleaned etc., at least every four months.

The gauge cocks to be blown through at least once a day. Not less than two inches of water should show in the gauge glass. The working

A swing bridge engine and driving gear for rotating and locking the bridge.

Chief Mechanical Engineer, British Rail, Swindon

pressure not to exceed sixty pounds per square inch.

A form recording the above work to be filled up daily.,

Only one set of turning and locking gear to be used and to be changed every four months.

The locking indicator to be tested and adjusted, if needed, every three days.

When the Bridge is locked the indicator pointer should be opposite the top mark, and the test marks on the locking gear opposite each other.

The ends of the Bridge must be examined about mid-day each day to see that the signal plungers and pawls are clear, and if any adjustment is necessary it must be reported to the signal lineman. If the ends of the rails touch or the space be too much, it must be reported to the Inpsector or ganger of permanent way.

A record must be kept of the numbers of hours worked by the reservoir donkey pump in each day and sent at the end of each month to the Clerk of the Works.

The surface of water in reservoir is not to be lower than six inches below the overflow.

Technical terms

Pitching

The term used for the rough quarried stone deposited around the bases of the piers to firm in the foundations. In 1880, 27,300 tons of pitching was deposited around all piers with the exception of pier number one.

An early attempt was made to carry out this operation from the bridge permanent way, but the method was abandoned and barges were used to transport the stone to the bridge site.

Scouring

The action of the tidal eddies around the bases of the piers across the Ridge resulted in a deep circular depression, unusually large depressions were filled in with pitching.

Banding

Prior to his retirement early in the twentieth century, Keeling was greatly concerned at the amount of cracks appearing with alarming regularity in the pier cylinders of the bridge, and also regarding the problem of corrosion.

The pier sections were repaired by bolting wrought iron bands around the defective sections, spare pier cylinders at Lydney Motive Power Deport were used as templates for rolling the bands.

Keeling's fears regarding corrosion were without foundation. in 1960, following the tanker accident, samples of cast iron were removed from the stump of pier number seventeen and tests showed the material to be of a low quality cast iron (seven point five tons to the square inch) but was free from graphitisation caused by the action of sea water.

Navigation lights

The navigation lights were displayed from dusk until dawn and were in the form of a white light on both sides of pier number twenty-one, a red light on both sides of pier number twenty and a white light on both sides of pier number nineteen.

Originally, oil burning lights were converted to electricity in 1959 with forty watt bulbs supplying the illumination, duplicate circuits were provided with an automatic change over switch in case of failure.

Gramme Machine

A dynamo or generating set. The term Gramme machine was derived from Gramme ring which refers to the type of windings used in the generator.

Index

Numbers in italic refer to illustrations.

Fishing industry and trade, 21, 23
Fitzhardinge, F., *2nd Baron*, 15–23
Floodlighting, 46
Forest of Dean, 5, 10, 11, 16, 19, 25,
    43, 56, 76, 78, 84, 150
    Coalfields, 17–23, 24, 68 et seq., 93,
        95
    Freeminers, 91
    Iron ore fields, 18, 23, 24
    Strikes and starvation, 68 et seq.
Forest of Dean Central Railway, 11, 34
Fortt, R., 57
Foster, T.N., 24, 29
Foundation stone laid, 29
Fowler, John, 5, 6, 9, 10
Framilode, 20, 54
    Passage, 1
France, R.L., 126
Francillon, J.C., *101*
Francis, T.C., 120
Freeman, R.W., 24
Fretherne, 4
Fripp, Stewart, 86, 107
Frocester, 9
Fulljames, Thomas, 5
Fulton, Hamilton H., 5

Garston, 30, 32, *41*
Gas pipeline, Sharpness-Lydney, 121
Gatcombe (Berkeley), 9, 54, 55, 65
Gibson, Milner, 7
Giles, W., 102
Gloster Aircraft Co. (Firm), *141*
Gloucester, 1, 3, 6, 10, 11, 16, 24, 25,
    30, 32, 50, 56, 57, 63, 69, 71, 84,
    101, 107, 112, 123, 126, 144, 151
Gloucester and Berkeley Canal, 9, 13,
    14, 25, 28, *38*, 144
    Company, 7, 15–23, 26, 48, 57, 76,
        87, 96
Gloucester and Birmingham Naviga-
    tion Co., 40, 92
Gloucester and Sharpness Steam
    Packet Co., *101*
Gloucester Banking Company, 108
Gloucester Chamber of Commerce, 6,
    7, 13, 16, 57
Gloucester Commissioner of Sewers,
    15–23
Gloucester Corporation, 6, 16, 57, 108
Gloucester High Level Bridge, 7, 8, 9,
    10

Gloucester *Journal* (newspaper), 1, 5,
    10, 52
Gloucester Over Bridge, 115
Gloucestershire County Council, 105,
    108
Golden Valley Railway, 104
Gooch, Sir Daniel, 57, 61, 63
Gordon, – (Colonel), 126
Gough, K., 112
Gower, John, 20
Gramme machine, 46, 162
Grange Class locomotives, 110
Great Western and Midland Consulta-
    tive Committee, 100
Great Western Railway, 5, 9, 10, 11,
    24, 25, 26, 34, 43, 48, 56, 57, 60,
    61, 63, 75, 84, 89, 104, 110
    Acquires Bridge Railway, 98–109,
    Declines to take up take up bridge
    shares, 27, Objects to Severn
    Bridge, 15–23
Grierson, J., 22
Griffey, D., 131
Griffiths, Griffith, 45, 48, 57, *142*, 150

Hagloe Park, 34
Halesowen Railway Joint Committee,
    100
Hall Class locomotives, 110
Hamburg, 131
Hamiltons Windsor Iron Works Co
    (Firm), 29, 30, 32, 40, *41*, 44, 45,
    50, 57, 60, 61, 70
Hardy, W. (Boatowner), 146
Hardy, W. (Driver), 122, 123
Harker, John, *Ltd.* (Firm), 123
Harms, Ulrich, 128, et seq
Harris, V., 145, 146
Harrison, Thomas Elliott, 19, 39, 60
Hart, M., 120
Hartnell, H.W., 84
Hathaway, W., 88
Hawkins, – (Relieving officer), 95
Hearne, J.P., 6
Hereford, 2
Hereford Journal (newspaper), xi
Hetheridge, Henry, 21
High Court of Justice, Admiralty Divi-
    sion, 123
Hobrough, W.F., 48
Hook Crib, 1, 4, 6

166

169

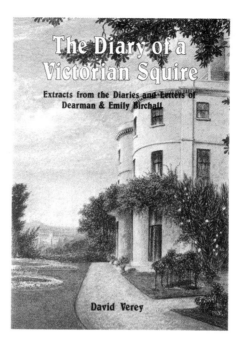

The Diary of a Victorian Squire

David Verey

Dearman Birchall,
Edited by David Verey

This is the story of a Quaker cloth merchant from Leeds, who bought a country house in Gloucestershire and became integrated with the Victorian squirarchy. Magistrate, Alderman, and in due course High Sheriff, Dearman Birchall pursued the fashionable life, the season in London and the winter abroad. His brilliant wife's letters home on their six-month wedding tour, and later from Moscow and Gibraltar are outstanding features of the book. We get fascinating glimpses of their interior decorator Aldam Heaton, the aesthetic movement, and their acquaintances Matthew Arnold and Oscar Wilde, as well as the servant problem, the pleasure of tricycling, and their country neighbours Thomas Gambier Parry, St. John Ackers, Bishop Ellicott and the rest.

Squire Birchall became a pillar of the established church; at the same time he was a great china-collector, art connoisseur, theatre-goer and ladies' man. This book provides a delightful insight into everyday upper class family life in Victorian times and is edited by the squire's grandson David Verey who has written explanatory notes throughout.

224pp 219mm x 157mm
Illustrated
ISBN 0 86299 055 6 (cloth) £8.95
ISBN 0 86299 048 3 (paper) £5.95

The above prices are current (June 1984) and are subject to alteration.

SOVEREIGN

THE CANAL BOATMEN
1760–1914

HARRY HANSON

The Canal Boatmen
1760-1914

Harry Hanson

Harry Hanson here discusses the economic and social condition of the Canal people against the background of the developing canal system and its eventual decline under the impact of the railway age. He offers evidence challenging existing beliefs on the origins of the boatmen and the importance of the 'Number One', and reveals when the 'family' boat first became widespread. The life style of the boatmen is studied from contemporary descriptions and he shows how a distinctive waterway sub-culture developed through the nineteenth century. An attempt is made to establish how much truth there was in the allegations that drunkenness, violence and immorality flourished on board the narrow boats.

The book will be of interest to transport and social historians of the nineteenth century as well as to the general reader. A number of rare photographs are included, together with extensive statistical appendices.

Sovereign
256pp 219mm x 157mm
Illustrated
ISBN 0 86299 067 X (paper) £5.95

The above price is current (June 1984) and is subject to alteration.

Stroudwater & Thames and Severn Canals Towpath Guide

Michael Handford and David Viner

The Cotswolds are widely recognised as one of the most attractive and visited areas in southern England. The main canals in the region, the Stroudwater and the Thames and Severn Canals, cross the Cotswolds from west to east and penetrate some of the most beautiful countryside in England, including picturesque areas such as the Golden Valley at Chalford.

Built between 1775 and 1789, the two canals are thirty-seven miles long with fifty-seven locks. Their more interesting features include the impressive group of locks climbing steeply from Stroud, and the famous Sapperton Tunnel, which at about two and a quarter miles long is the third longest canal tunnel ever built in England.

This walking guide takes its readers along the towpath pointing out the main features with the help of photographs, line illustrations and maps.

224pp 219mm x 157mm
Illustrated
ISBN 0 904387 61 5 (paper) £4.95

The above price is current (June 1984) and is subject to alteration.

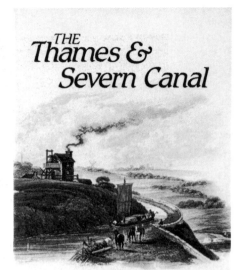

THE
Thames &
Severn Canal

Humphrey Household

The Thames and Severn Canal

Humphrey Household

2nd Edition, revised with additional photographs.

The Thames & Severn Canal stretched from Inglesham, near Lechlade on the Upper Thames, to Stroud where it joined the Stroudwater Navigation leading to the Severn at Framilode.

It was the fulfilment of one of the earliest, perhaps the earliest, of all proposals to link British river navigations by an artificial waterway crossing the water-shed and when built in 1783-1789 it had the longest and largest tunnel in the world.

Its archives in the Gloucestershire Record Office are exceptional, probably unique, in the wealth of material bearing on the engineering and construction, the carrying trade and provision of boats, the management and operation of a canal in the late eighteenth and nineteenth centuries and in the long struggle to maintain the concern in the face of decreasing trade and falling revenue.

Some twenty years of research led to the production of the first edition of this history in 1969 and the description of that as 'a thorough, well-written and unusually wide-ranging study of a water-way' is evidently justified by the demand for a second edition, enlarged and with far more illustrations, in this year of the bicentenary of the Act incorporating the company.

258pp 219mm x 157mm
Illustrated
ISBN 0 86299 056 4 (cloth) £9.95

The above price is current (June 1984) and is subject to alteration.

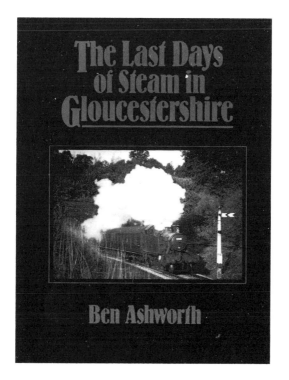

The Last Days of Steam in Gloucestershire

Ben Ashworth

This is a photographic record of the railways of Gloucestershire during a revolutionary period, between 1959 and 1966. In 1959, steam power was still pre-eminent, branch lines were still operating and stations and halts were many. By 1966, diesel power had usurped the steam locomotive, most branch lines were closed and only a small number of stations remained in use. Over 200 superbly atmospheric photographs capture this era of major change to provide a permanent record of interest to the railway buff, social historian, indeed anyone who loves steam trains.

144pp 246mm x 186mm
Illustrated
ISBN 0 86299 057 2 (cloth) £7.95

The above price is current (June 1984) and is subject to alteration.